What a journey, what a life! Chandrakant Shah is a towering figure in Canadian Public Health. In addition to mentoring scores of colleagues, trainees, and students over the course of his impressive career, his work has far-reaching impact on not just health policy, but also broader social issues, especially those relating to inequalities, discrimination, and marginalization.

—Kue Young, Professor Emeritus, Dalla Lana School of Public Health, University of Toronto, and former Dean, School of Public Health, University of Alberta

To Change the World intertwines the personal and professional stories of a Canadian physician with a relentless commitment to improvement and equity. Chandrakant Shah's passionate story shows a model Canadian story of an immigrant physician who wins professional success while focusing on making the country more inclusive and more just. His story is a good remedy for these cynical and polarized times.

—Adalsteinn Brown, Dean, Dalla Lana School of Public Health, University of Toronto

This book imparts what it means to understand and support Indigenous health in Canada. Chandrakant Shah's intellect and sense of humour shed light on every topic he touches. His story will entrain, inform, and sometimes shock readers; this is an important text in public health that aims to shift the discourse and the paradigm.

—Suzanne Stewart, Director of the Waakebiness-Bryce Institute for Indigenous Health, Dalla Lana School of Public Health, University of Toronto

To *Change* *the* World

My Work With
Diversity,
Equity
&
Inclusion
in Canada

Chandrakant P Shah

MAWENZI
HOUSE

Published with the generous assistance of the Canada Council for the Arts and the Ontario Arts Council. We also acknowledge the support of the Government of Canada through the Canada Book Fund and the Government of Ontario through the Ontario Book Publishing Tax Credit.

Cover design by Sabrina Pignataro
Cover image: Lightspring/Multi cultural society and multiculturalism as a celebration of diverse cultures and diversity or multicultural social unity with people of different races united in a 3D illustration style/Shutterstock

Library and Archives Canada Cataloguing in Publication

Title: To change the world : my work with diversity, equity & inclusion in Canada / Chandrakant P Shah.

Names: Shah, Chandrakant P. (Chandrakant Padamshi), 1936- author.

Description: Includes bibliographical references and index.

Identifiers: Canadiana (print) 20230524400 | Canadiana (ebook) 20230524508 | ISBN 9781774151099 (softcover) | ISBN 9781774151105 (EPUB) | ISBN 9781774151112 (PDF)

Subjects: LCSH: Shah, Chandrakant P. (Chandrakant Padamshi), 1936- | LCSH: Public health personnel—Canada—Biography. | LCSH: Physicians—Canada—Biography. | LCSH: Discrimination in medical care—Canada. | LCSH: Indigenous peoples—Medical care—Canada. | LCSH: Public health—Canada. | LCSH: Rural health—Canada. | LCSH: Health services accessibility—Canada. | LCGFT: Autobiographies.

Classification: LCC RA424.5.S53 A3 2023 | DDC 362.1092—dc23

Printed and bound in Canada by Coach House Printing

Mawenzi House Publishers Ltd.
39 Woburn Avenue (B)
Toronto, Ontario M5M 1K5
Canada

www.mawenzihouse.com

To my late parents Surajben and Padamshi for teaching me the dignity of human life; my wife Sudha, my sons Sunil and Rajiv, my granddaughters Anita and Neha, for their unwavering support in my all endeavours; and the Indigenous peoples of Canada for accepting me as their ally in my journey towards reconciliation.

Never doubt that a small group of thoughtful, committed citizens can change the world; indeed, it's the only thing that ever has.

MARGARET MEAD

Contents

Foreword

Dr Chandrakant Shah has lived many lives, navigating countless challenges while transforming the lives of many in his storied personal and professional life. This memoir takes us on a journey from his humble beginnings in India to a life of extraordinary achievements that have benefited all Canadians.

Growing up in a large family in a small rural community in India, Dr Shah, as a member of India's Jain faith shares the spiritual goal of becoming liberated from the endless cycle of rebirths to achieve an all-knowing state called Moksha. It is here that his work with the Indigenous community in Toronto and Ontario intersects seamlessly with the Indigenous Seven Grandfather Teachings of wisdom, bravery, honesty, respect, truth, humility and love. His many years of work with the Indigenous community embodies his passion for justice and kindness. Dr Shah practiced reconciliation long before it became a national endeavour. His championing of Indigenous cultural safety in Ontario's colleges and universities, and his supporting and developing the Urban Indigenous Health Strategy, besides fighting racism, highlight only a few of his enormous contributions to Indigenous well-being.

This masterful memoir animates his words in such a manner that it feels as though he is personally telling us the remarkable story of his life. He gives us a roadmap sharing his challenges and successes: enlightening the Citizenship Test, the importance of culturally safe public health care, public health, advocating for children and the disabled, writing the Canadian Public Health Care textbook with the help of his elder son Sunil, and the patience of his best friend and greatest supporter, his loving wife Sudha. The list of his struggles and accomplishments makes a compelling read.

Dr Shah has a proud refrain that echoes through the pages of this heartfelt book – "*a former student of mine.*" The list of his accomplished students is literally a Who's Who of the Canadian health establishment, with men and women who have led Canada through various medical crises.

Dr Shah was given the Indigenous Spirit name Maamaazhii N'iamh Manidoo Aki, meaning "conquered his Spirit on earth," because when you conquer your spirit on earth you truly know who you are. Dr Shah knows who he is. In the pages of this remarkable memoir we all are welcomed through his indomitable spirit to become his "former students."

Andre Morriseau
Chair, Board of Directors
Anishnawbe Health Foundation
Communications Manager, Ontario Native Women's Association

Introduction

As a South Asian immigrant from India who began his career as a pediatrician in Canada in the 1960s and transitioned into the field of public health, my journey has been adventurous. This book is an attempt at sharing with you, my dear reader, the highs and lows of a life dedicated to the cause of Canada's most vulnerable population—the Indigenous people of this land. It is also the story of my work with the other underprivileged populations of this country, such as the poor, the homeless, the unemployed, and the visible minorities; it involved unimaginable challenges and battles that—I believe—most would have shunned.

As a public health practitioner, when I tried to influence social changes that would improve the health of Canada's vulnerable groups, I met many hurdles related to the fact that I was a first-generation immigrant belonging to a visible minority; I was not well-connected, and this also made a big difference. But none of these reasons was strong enough to stray me from the path that I had chosen. There were a number of factors from my early life such as the Jain faith and its teachings of nonviolence (*ahimsa*), respect for nature, and forgiveness and tolerance; witnessing the independence movement of India, which showed me the importance of self-determination for nations (decolonization and reconciliation); Gandhi's struggles against discrimination, which gave me the conviction to do what was right. I will describe the influence of my Jain faith and Mahatma Gandhi in a later chapter.

I have always valued this quotation attributed to Margaret Mead: "Never doubt that a small group of thoughtful, committed citizens can change the world; indeed, it's the only thing that ever has." In our society, we are constantly reminded of changes—some due to technology; some to globalization; and others to the work of social activists. Changes are generally slow to occur. However, once implemented, they profoundly affect humanity. I have never believed in being simply a bystander, one among the silent majority, who thinks that things will change with time and would rather wait for someone else to take the initiative. I took the initiatives. I may be part of a so-called visible minority, but whenever I was convinced that a change was needed that would significantly positively impact the lives of people, I tried my best to make it happen. For all the privileges I have been bestowed with, I feel it is my duty to "move beyond good intentions,"—a belief and an action plan that I have sworn by all my adult life.

Sir Wilfrid Laurier dreamt of Canada as a Gothic Cathedral: "I want the marble to remain the marble, the granite to remain the granite, the oak to remain the oak—and out of all these elements, I would build a nation great among the nations of the world." My vision of Canada as multicultural was shaped by Laurier's dream. In my heart, I too wanted to see in a predominantly white culture the Black people retaining their heritage, the East Asians retaining their East Asian heritage; the South Asians retaining their South Asian heritage; the First Nations retaining their First Nations' heritage; the Inuit retaining their Inuit heritage; and Métis retaining their Métis heritage. I want to see Canada become a shining example of diversity and inclusion. This is my dream. But that reality, as we all know, is not easily achieved.

The COVID-19 pandemic and the Black Lives Matter movement following the death of George Floyd in the United States have further exposed social inequality even in the so called most "developed" nations of the world. This is proved by the fact that it is the poor, the immigrant, the "racialized," the homeless, the Indigenous, and the elderly who've had higher rates of infection and deaths. Systemic racism in all our institutions also surfaced its ugly head. Having devoted my life to fight this inhuman prejudice and with the hope that many will join hands with me to keep the efforts going, I felt this to be the right moment to write about my decades-long efforts in the field to illustrate what a painfully slow but satisfying process influencing social change can be, and the need for a sustained commitment. My story is long, but the devil lies in the details—to pull out a cliché. It is my love for the smallest things that perhaps gave me the strength and patience to overcome long, hard battles. But the victories that follow bitterest battles are the sweetest.

1

From Modest Beginnings . . . Stepping Out

I was born in 1936 in Nandurbar (then with a population of approximately 30,000) in the state of Maharashtra, India. In 1911, my father had emigrated to Nandurbar from the state of Gujarat (the birthplace of Mahatma Gandhi, Prime Minister Narendra Modi, and Pakistan's Mohammed Ali Jinnah) for work. My father had lost his own father when he was seven years old. As the eldest son, he had to take on family responsibilities after finishing high school at the young age of seventeen, even though he was offered a scholarship by the government to study further. He began his career as a bookkeeper in a ginning factory and quickly grasped the intricacies of the cotton trade, which led him to establish his own cotton business with a partner who supplemented his creativity and talent with the requisite capital.

The ninth among fifteen children, I had eight sisters and six brothers. My father was previously married and had lost his first wife in childbirth leaving behind two sons and two daughters. My father remarried and had eleven children with my mother. None of us ever uttered once the fact that we had stepbrothers and stepsisters; all were treated equally. Many of our closest friends did not know that we had stepsiblings. No doubt at times there was tension in the family, but as I reflect about it, this was largely due to living closely in a relatively small house (four rooms and a kitchen for fifteen or more of us), with limited financial resources. As his sons grew up, they joined his business, but when they got married, they had their families to support, and the elder sons with their families moved out and lived in separate dwellings.

My father was a well-read man; he even had his own small library. His English was impeccable (so it seemed then), and he would even correct my English correspondence later in his life. Evening was the time when we saw him, since during the daytime he would be busy earning livelihood for such a large family. He was considered a wise man in our town and every evening from six to eight we had a string of visitors sitting in our veranda, asking for his advice on various issues. During this period, his younger sons took turns to massage his lower limbs, since he suffered from leg cramps. We could not talk but just listened. I believe I absorbed many good values and principles from listening to these evening encounters. He also was a disciplinarian; I suppose he had to be, to keep order in the house with so many children. In the later stage of his life, when we were older, none of us ever thought to disobey or challenge him even when we knew he was wrong.

Since her marriage at the age of seventeen, my mother was burdened with running a large household with four young stepchildren under six years of age besides her own large number. She had accepted her fate and did her duty to raise and marry all her children and even some of her grandchildren and great-grandchildren. Though she had only primary school education, she absorbed a lot from her surroundings and to my utter surprise, when she visited us in Canada, she could grasp the gist of our English conversations. Three of my brothers as well as three of my sisters managed to graduate from university. As my brothers started having their own families, my father had to diversify his business in several directions, becoming the owner of a grain shop, a hardware store, and a drug store. Like all siblings, no doubt we fought with each other and there were family squabbles, but we had to learn how to share and care for each other. The older sisters and sisters-in-law had to care for the younger ones and were almost mother surrogates, my mother's hands being too full; similarly at times the elder brothers served as father surrogates. Therefore, we formed strong family bonds.

My middle-class family valued education, but my parents never pushed us to excel. I was expected to join my father's business after I finished high school. When I was growing up, Nandurbar had one primary school, one middle school, and two high schools, one where the language of instruction was Marathi, which was the language of Maharashtra State, and the other where it was Gujarati and which I attended. The availability of electricity and telephone was minimal; my home had neither. I remember studying in the evenings with the help of a floodlight from the restaurant next door and at nighttime I studied under a kerosene lamp in our kitchen, the only quiet sanctuary available in a noisy household. With barely any place to sit down and study in peace during the daytime, I sought refuge in the tiny, dingy storage room at the back of our shop, perched on top of sacks of grain or in an isolated warehouse owned by our business partners. I had to walk three kilometres each way to school, six days a week. I always stood first in my class academically and even received a gold medal upon graduation.

Since Nandurbar lacked facilities for higher education, after graduating from high school in 1961 I went to Surat, in the State of Gujarat, the closest large city, for my premedical studies. At that time, I felt I was lucky to even attend university. While I had heard of prestigious colleges like Elphinstone College and Wilson College in Mumbai, I believed that they were beyond my reach. In

Surat I had my best friend from high school, Jaswant, and several others from Nandurbar, and their companionship helped me avoid loneliness.

For medical school I went to the BJ Medical College in Ahmedabad. I was a reasonably good medical student, but I had little aptitude for sports. I was a total nerd. In Ahmedabad, I did not know anyone except two distant relatives. Ahmedabad was a very large metropolis with the typical hustle and bustle of a large city. There was the general impression that Ahmedabadis in general and my fellow students from Ahmedabad in general were too stingy to invite anyone to their homes. I was lonely and starved for family life. Luckily, a fellow student called Ashwin Pandya became my friend, and his generous family adopted me as their son. Till today, many of his family members who have emigrated to the United States consider me as one of them.

After I graduated from BJ Medical College, I did my postgraduate training in internal medicine as a resident for six months in the Civic Hospital, also in Ahmedabad. I did not participate in organized activities, but I developed a very close circle of both male and female friends, most of them ending up in the US, where they keep in touch with each other. College life consisted mainly of studying and outings to restaurants or cinemas, which were not very frequent. All my friends came from middle-income families with limited resources. Among us were South Asian students from Kenya and Uganda, however, who lived lavish lifestyles and were the envy of others. During this period, I learned that America admitted foreign-trained physicians for further training at their hospitals as interns and residents and paid rather well. Our friend Ravi's elder sister had returned from America and painted a very rosy picture of the place.

The British profoundly shaped many spheres of Indian life,

including academics and the political system. Influences of the British Raj persisted in India for years after its independence. At that time in India, a postgraduate degree and diploma from Britain were highly valued—but not from America. My friends Ravi and Pankaj were planning to go to UK for further studies, and Ashwin and his brother Shirish to the US and listening to their plans and discussions I was tempted also to pursue further studies abroad. While I was initially in a dilemma about where to go, I finally decided to pursue training in the United States and reached its shores in February 1962. My family—parents and older siblings— had mixed feelings about my going abroad; my father was totally against it. He had the feeling—how right he was!—that he would lose his son to the distant land for ever. I invited him to visit me in Ahmedabad, where I introduced him to Ashwin's mother, who convinced my father to let me go. She told him that despite her being a widow, she was still allowing her two sons to go abroad, where opportunities were better. Doctors were needed and respected in America. Why thwart a young man's ambition? She was willing to support my travel if he could not. With much reluctance he agreed. His other concern was about my being ten thousand kilometres away in a foreign land without any social support; learning that my friends would be close by (so he thought), he was partly relieved.

The United States—a Brief Stint (1962–1964)

I was accepted at St John Hospital, a community facility in Cleveland, Ohio. I arrived in the middle of winter and it was very cold; at night the roads were empty and ghostly, unlike the hustle and bustle of India. And yet the living conditions were so much better than in India. The major hurdle I faced was food. I was vegetarian, and in those days, vegetarians were a strange animal. All my meals were provided by the hospital, and they did not know what to do with me. I was provided a tray of cottage cheese and fruits seven days a week. I was so fed up with the cottage cheese that for many years afterwards, I would not deign to look at it. The nursing staff were good to me and occasionally took me for outings on my days off. It being a Catholic hospital, I saw nuns or priests doing the last rites for a dying patient. Once, when no nun or priest was available for a dying young child, I did the last rites. When a nun found out about this she was upset and asked me whether I had done Hindu last rites! I told her we did not have such a tradition and I had followed the Christian ritual.

I missed the stimulating atmosphere of the university hospital in Ahmedabad. Internal medicine was what I wanted to practice; however, at that time, in 1962, most patients in St John Hospital were old, with multiple health issues. Internal medicine in the US was entering a phase of geriatric care and I did not find it challenging enough. However, after some months I had a brief stint in the pediatric ward. I was energized and loved working with the sick children. I realized that pediatrics was my calling. I wanted to be trained at a university hospital and so I moved to the pediatrics program at Mercy Hospital which was affiliated with the Stritch School of Medicine at Loyola University, Chicago. It did not quite match my expectations, and the following year I moved yet again, to the University of Illinois's Teaching and Research Hospital, taking a junior resident position. Here I finally found what I was longing for—an excellent learning experience. Within two years, I acquired my diploma from the American Board of Pediatrics and in October of that year (1964) decided to go to Glasgow, Scotland to pursue a postgraduate degree that I believed would be more valued in India.

All Commonwealth countries valued UK qualification, and there were many students doing their "housemanship" (internship or residency) in smaller peripheral nonteaching hospitals which were shunned by British graduates. These places had virtually no teaching, hence, to pass their examinations, these students needed extra courses. There were many such courses available and the fees were exorbitant for foreigners—as a matter of fact, providing them became a very lucrative business for many teachers and sponsoring institutions. The success rate was around fifteen percent and many physicians taking these examinations from the Commonwealth countries succeeded only after several attempts. Luckily it took me only nine months to be certified in pediatrics and internal medicine by the Royal College of Physicians and Surgeons of Glasgow. I explored several academic venues in India in order to settle there but somehow nothing materialized. While I was strongly attached to my family and my country, India, I knew in my heart that I wanted to teach and practice in an academic setting, and such jobs were not available in India. I then decided to immigrate to Canada, reaching Vancouver in June 1965. My father was not pleased with my decision, but eventually came around and later was proud of my successful career.

Vancouver – Formative Years (1965–1972)

On my first trip back to India in 1966, I was introduced by a family friend to my future wife, Sudha, a general physician who practiced in Mumbai. Raised in a large metropolis, she was relatively fluent in English, outgoing, family oriented, and of the Jain faith. I was looking for a partner who would be compatible and integrate into Canadian society without much difficulty and I was happy to find her. A short courtship later, we were married and soon after, Sudha joined me in Vancouver. Unfortunately, Sudha encountered major difficulties in acquiring a license to practice in British Columbia. Her Indian degree was not recognized in British Columbia; she was asked to take her basic sciences examination following which she was required to do additional two years of undergraduate medical training. She was promised admittance by the dean of medicine at the University of British Columbia once she passed her basic sciences. But after passing basic sciences, she was interviewed by the dean, who told her to go home and raise her family. (She was pregnant at that time.) This was flagrant gender discrimination, but at the time there was no recourse to fight that. Needless to say, she was heart-broken and took many months to accept the fact that she would never be a doctor in Canada.

I chose Canada as I perceived it to be a country that was just and equitable. I had visited Niagara Falls, Ottawa, Montreal, and Quebec City for a week during my stay in the US and was impressed by Canada's political and social systems. In the early sixties, I would see discussions on US television about how communism was creeping up in Canada; this was in reference to the Canadian initiative for universal medical care insurance. In contrast, I thought Canada was moving in the right direction. During my brief vacations in Montreal and Quebec City, I had been impressed by the civility and cleanliness all over. I could walk at night without fear of being robbed. I felt safe.

However, the reality was more complex, as Sudha's ordeal shows. I experienced a significant amount of discrimination in my professional and personal life.

We bought a house in a middle-class all-white neighbourhood of Vancouver in 1970. None of our neighbours came to greet us, but a dentist's wife took the trouble to warn us that in *their* neighbourhood they maintained their lawns and were concerned whether we would be able to do so too. I had a mind to inform her that we had two goats who would do the job! Six months later, a few children of our white neighbours vandalized my backyard fence. I somehow managed to catch the culprits the very next day: eight of them confessed and one of them, along with his father, repaired the fence. Such was the atmosphere I had entered.

Eventually I established my credentials as a professional after training for another two years to acquire a licence to practice pediatrics as a fellow of the Royal College of Physicians and Surgeons of Canada. Being an academician at heart, private practice never appealed to me. In 1967, I began working as a clinical instructor at the University of British Columbia's Department of Pediatrics. I was very fortunate to work under the late Dr Geoffrey Robinson, a distinguished pediatrician who instilled in me an "inquiring mind," leading to research and communication, skills that I used in my journey towards humanizing health care. We went on to become close friends. But for his influence during my formative years in Canada, I am not sure which path I would have chosen.

My dedication to collect all the data round the clock as his work horse, with no previous experience in research, gained me new skills and a new way of thinking. It gave me an opportunity to develop proficiency in writing research grants and papers. Dr Robinson, who was by nature shy, assigned me the duty of presenting our research findings at national and international conferences, despite my poor command of English at the time. While I had studied English as a second language in India from grade eight onward, I had never learned proper grammar, and the teachers themselves were not fluent in English. And so, the opportunity to present papers and speak about them gave me a lot of confidence, besides improving my spoken English.

In 1970, after three years working for Dr Robinson, I felt I had learned enough to venture out and work as an independent professional. I applied for the newly created position of medical director at the Children's Aid Society of Vancouver and was successful. As a medical director, I had to set up a full-time clinic for foster children and youths under the child welfare agency and I also carried out some other mandated functions that I will detail in a later chapter.

On the family front, Sudha and I were still a young couple with limited resources other than the zeal to succeed. It was difficult for Sudha. She missed being a family doctor, she missed her patients, and she missed getting up every day, dressing up, and leaving home for work. She also missed her large family and circle of friends in Mumbai, who had also depended on her for medical advice. She had given up part of her identity. However, having been raised in a cosmopolitan city like Mumbai, she was relatively fluent in English and because of her outgoing nature, she easily made friends with other Indian families in Vancouver and became involved in cultural activities. For my part, by nature, I have always enjoyed entertaining friends and colleagues at our home, giving lavish dinners and grand parties; therefore, we nurtured a wide circle of wonderful friends. I also sponsored the youngest member of my family, my brother Yogesh, who landed in Canada in 1970. The friends and my brother were our support system.

We were blessed with two sons, Sunil in 1969 and Rajiv in 1971. Sudha took on the major burden of caring for them while I was busy at work. This was no easy feat, and I was perhaps oblivious to even notice how the home front was being managed.

Toronto – From Pediatrics to Public Health (1972–)

I had always intended to settle in Toronto; however, the College of Physicians and Surgeons of Ontario had plainly informed me without mincing words that my premedical undergraduate qualifications were unacceptable, even though the medical school I graduated from was on the World Health Organization (WHO) approved list, and despite my medical qualifications and postgraduate training in pediatrics and internal medicine from both the US and the UK. The only doctors licenced to practice medicine in Ontario, other than Canadian and American medical graduates, were those from the UK, Ireland, and the "white" commonwealth countries, South Africa, Australia, and New Zealand. (Forty-two years later, in 2007, the same licensing body gave me an Outstanding Physician of Ontario award.)

However, in December 1971 I received a letter of offer for a professorship in his department by Dr Robert Morgan who had worked before as a consultant on my province-wide epidemiology study. He had been appointed as the Chair of the newly formed Department of Preventive Medicine in the Faculty of Medicine at the University of Toronto. When he was leaving Vancouver for Toronto in June 1971, I had casually mentioned to him that if he found a suitable job for me, I would be happy to consider moving to Toronto, as I had always considered Toronto as a major hub for research and teaching child health. I was pleasantly surprised with this unexpected letter of offer. While I had contributed significantly to child-health policies in British Columbia, this was a big step for me. I had never been formally trained in the field of public health, having always considered myself a pediatrician. I had focused my entire undergraduate and graduate schooling on individual patients' health and not with the health of larger populations and trends in their health status that public health dealt with. Much, if not all, of my experience in public health was from my previous epidemiological study at the Children's Aid Society in Vancouver. That experience largely consisted of learning the ropes as I went along.

As an undergraduate medical student in India, I had looked down on the field of public health (as did most of my fellow medical students), greatly undervaluing its importance. Historically, "real doctors" are known to be averse to it because it was mainly associated with subjects like sanitation, drinking water, immunization, etc, and not "real patients" with symptoms. The general impression that held sway amongst the medical community was that one entered public health only if one had no other choice. The brightest in medicine were expected to enter prestigious specialties like surgery and internal medicine or one of their subspecialties like orthopedics, plastic surgery, cardiology, and neurology. This obviously led to a dearth of professionals in public health and severely underdeveloped undergraduate and graduate programs at universities.

Now here I was, with an offer. Never in my wildest dreams had I imagined that a very casual and short conversation would change the trajectory of my life so drastically!

Intrigued by the opportunity and lured by the Hospital for Sick Children, which was world famous, I decided to accept the offer if it met two conditions. First, I would be affiliated with the Hospital for Sick Children, spending some time practicing pediatrics. The pediatric community already knew me from my work in Vancouver in the field of child welfare. As the Hospital for Sick Children lacked the expertise in the type of research I was involved in, they were happy to appoint me. Indeed, I was given a cross-appointment in the Department of Pediatrics and the Hospital for Sick Children.

My second condition was that the university would provide me with an opportunity to study a public health graduate program within the first two years of my appointment. While my wishes were granted, what should have been a matter of pride and exultation for me was instead laced with self-doubt. These were still early days of my career . . . and perhaps the stepping-stones to a future full of passionate advocacy for change.

I was quite apprehensive about receiving my practice license in Ontario, as I had been so blatantly refused before because of my Indian medical degree. However, both Dr Morgan and Dr Bain, who was head of pediatrics at the Hospital for Sick Children, assured me that I need not worry—they would make sure I received my license in Ontario. Spurred by their assurances, I accepted the offer and joined the newly created Department of Preventive Medicine at the Faculty of Medicine, University of Toronto, in July 1972. Sudha, while happy for the progress I was making in my career, was apprehensive about the move. She had made many friends and acquaintances in Vancouver, and another move in five years was too much to adjust to. For the first three months in Toronto, she found it difficult. She was often in tears. Fortunately, in our previous visit to Toronto we had met an Iranian faculty member from the School of Hygiene (Public Health) and a fellow pediatrician, Dr Hossein Moghadam and his wife Hilda, a Swedish nurse, who ended up becoming our lifeline.

Hilda was a wonderful and most efficient woman, always ready to help. She organized a real-estate agent for us and within a week we bought a house in the northwest part of Toronto where they resided. For the first three months, while I was meeting many new people, I was very excited. However, after those three months, I started missing my friends from Vancouver and what the city had to offer. At that time, I wondered whether we had made the right move.

Ours was a middle-class neighbourhood. But at that time, in the early seventies, Canada was perhaps going through one of its worst phases of racial discrimination and hatred. South Asian refugees had arrived from Uganda and there was an influx from the other East African countries. "Paki bashing" was not uncommon. While most of our neighbours were friendly, we were not spared the occasional incidents of hostility. Once a small explosive was placed on our front yard. Another time, our car, with my two young children in it, was deliberately pushed into a corner by another vehicle.

In the fall of 1973, I went to study at the Harvard School of Public Health's graduate program. I received a small grant for support during my study, and surprisingly, the Hospital for Sick Children paid my tuition fee. Most physicians usually enroll in the Master of Public Health program; however, I enrolled in the Master of Health Administration to study health care delivery systems. While I was enrolled as a graduate student in the Faculty of Public Health, I was also appointed as an assistant professor in pediatrics at the Harvard Medical School and a courtesy staff physician at the famous Boston Children's Hospital. For a person with such humble beginnings as mine, in a small village in India, working in such esteemed institutions was much beyond what I had dreamt of.

Going back to school and writing exams and term papers was not easy. I would consider this period to be the early days of a long career, one that was fraught with challenges galore. It was not just I who faced challenges. While I struggled with studying and taking exams, Sudha and the two young children lived in a small apartment in an international students' residence in the Roxbury area, which is known to be a rough neighbourhood. The area was so crime-ridden that we were required to have three different locks on our residential unit door even though there were security locks at our building's front entrance.

One of my American classmates was robbed in the middle of the day on a nearby street, when he went strolling with his young daughter accompanied by my older six-year-old son Sunil. We lived in perennial fear. Sometimes, when I look back, it amazes me to think of how my wife and kids survived those days. I was so busy with my studies and work that perhaps I never had the luxury to let fear get the better of me. I do think I am fortunate to have been blessed with a family that has always been supportive and resilient. If home meant living in a neighbourhood known for crime, school wasn't a bed of roses either!

I went to Harvard, expecting that the world-renowned academicians there would teach me—that was my thinking with my rose-tinted glasses on! Soon enough, I was given a reality check that

18

brought me crashing down! Far from being guided by these famous teachers, we hardly got an opportunity to even see them because they were busy with congressional hearings and lecturing worldwide, doing their research, or consulting. Most of my learning happened because of the interactions with my excellent fellow students. While the first term was fraught with struggles of becoming again a student, I realized that human beings are incredibly adaptive. Initial setback and bumps on the road soon gave way to making new friends and acquaintances; life in the student residence was in some way a blessing, since all of us were in a similar situation. We attended the world-renowned Boston Pops Orchestra in downtown Boston where you couldn't dare go alone at nighttime; we would therefore always pile up in a car with fellow students.

After completion of my degree in health administration in June 1974, I returned to Toronto. Back in Canada we felt relief—despite the racial and other problems, we felt fortunate that we were citizens of a largely peaceful county where we did not have to worry about guns, getting robbed, or going anywhere after dark! I almost kissed the soil of my adopted motherland.

My first personal encounter with inequity and discrimination in Canada occurred at the home front in 1980, at the University of Toronto. Along with a white woman and a Chinese professor, I was under consideration for a promotion from associate to full professor. The chairman of the department failed to follow procedure and promoted the white professor even though she had risen only the previous year from assistant to associate professor. The Chinese professor and I had been kept waiting for six years. It usually takes an average of five to seven years and many publications to be promoted to full professor. I wondered whether this was racism on the part of the chairman and the committee.

We appealed on the grounds of a flawed process. Fortunately, the judging process was repeated from scratch and all three of us we were promoted to full professors. I will never forget getting the call I received at home to tell me the news.

Meanwhile . . .

In 1987 the medical licencing body in Ontario proposed to change their by-laws prohibiting internationally trained physicians who were already Canadian citizens from moving from other provinces to Ontario. This again was a blatant case of discrimination—under this by-law I would never have made it to Toronto with my Indian degrees! The proposed change would violate Freedom of Mobility as laid out in the Canadian Charter of Rights, so I filed an official complaint to the Ontario Human Right Commission. I contacted many internationally trained physicians "of colour" for their support, but while they were willing to support the cause financially, they were not willing to put their names forward for fear of reprisals from the licencing body. Two brave foreign-born physicians, Dr Olivia Chung-James, and another whose name I may not reveal here, did join my cause. The Human Rights Tribunal of Ontario heard my complaint and asked the College of Physicians and Surgeons of Ontario to rescind the by-law. This was the first amongst many of the tiny steps I found myself taking towards standing up for what I believed was right. While each step seemed daunting at first, as John Burroughs once said, "Leap and the net will appear."

Bringing about change, whether it is at the personal or societal level, is difficult, at best slow, and sometimes impossible—the hurdles are so large. Good intentions only are not sufficient; it is sustained commitment over a long period that brings about change. I learned not to quit easily; perhaps it was a dormant quality in me that emerged in Canada. You may lose a battle or two, but the war must be won. You could still fail, but that is the time to reflect and learn lessons on why you failed and to be humble.

2

Working With Indigenous Communities

Upon my return from Harvard in 1974, I became involved with the Sioux Lookout Zone Program in Northwestern Ontario by volunteering my pediatric services. (The Zone is at a Latitude of approximately 50° North.) This program was established in 1967 by the late Dr Harry Bain, pediatrician-in-chief at the Hospital for Sick Children, and provided health services to remote Indigenous First Nations communities. I had never met any Indigenous people before and knew very little about them. I was driven to offer my services initially out of curiosity to learn about Indigenous people and a sense of adventure, the thrill to see a remote part of Canada. In time, when I had seen their lack of health care, their poor living conditions, the threat to their cultures and languages, I began to understand their demands for self-determination. I felt I could be of some direct help if I were to provide health care for children, who constituted almost fifty percent of their population. I also had the tools and voice to publicize their cause by doing relevant research and advocating for them.

The Sioux Lookout Zone is a large, sparsely populated area in Northwest Ontario, inhabited by First Nations Peoples in twenty-six very remote communities accessible by small aircraft. At that time, the size of the communities ranged from 250 to 1,600 people, totalling 16,000. (Now it is over 33,000). The area was as undeveloped as a remote village in India. The houses were often prefabricated modules brought from the south without any consideration for the harsh northern climate. They were poorly constructed and heated by wood-burning stoves and lacked indoor plumbing and toilets. Infrastructures such as road, electricity, and potable water were nonexistent; there were a nursing station, a school, and living quarters for nurses, visiting doctors and teachers. In many cases multigeneration families lived in two to three bedrooms. These crowded situations caused lots of stress in individual family members and provided fertile ground for the transmission of infectious diseases.

Organization of Health Services for Remote First Nations Communities

Under the Canadian Constitution, the federal government is responsible for the health of First Nations People living on a reserve, and the provincial government for the rest of its population. The town of Sioux Lookout (population 3500 in 1970s) was a hub for providing health services to both its local population and the First Nations communities in the north. It had two hospitals, one operated by the province and the other by the federal government and known as the Sioux Lookout Zone Hospital (SLZH). The latter provided primary health care and hospital care to all twenty-six communities in the north. Due to the remoteness of these communities and the lack of support services, it was always difficult to recruit and retain physicians and nurses to provide health services, thus there was chronic shortage and suboptimal health care for First Nations communities. Those who worked there knew little about history, culture, language, belief systems and traditional healing practices of their patients.

Communities with populations of over 500 had a health station staffed by one or two nurses and an itinerant physician who flew in for three to five days every four to six weeks. Smaller communities had health stations staffed by a local community health worker, trained to administer first aid and treat minor ailments, and were visited by a nurse once a month and a physician every four to six weeks. If a patient needed to be monitored or assessed frequently, for example for diabetes, they were required to move to larger communities. All pregnant women in their last 8–12 weeks were transferred to the Sioux Lookout Zone Hospital, located sometimes hundreds of kilometres away from their home, without any family support. These women left behind their young children and husbands and always worried about them. Emergency patients were evacuated by medivac.

Realizing this sorry state of affairs, the Faculty of Medicine of the University of Toronto and the Hospital for Sick Children had signed a contract in 1967 with the Federal Government to provide physicians and allied health care professional services to these communities. As it provided a unique opportunity to work in remote communities, it was a very popular program for medical students and residents. In our zeal to serve, we ignored certain basic tenets of doctor-patient relationships. Many older people in the community did not speak English and local staff acted as interpreters, compromising patient privacy. Health care professionals at that time did not receive any training in cultural sensitivity or safety and did not know even a smattering of Indigenous history or the impact of their colonization. In retrospect, we were ignorant, with our inherent biases and attitudes towards the people we were serving.

I visited the Sioux Lookout Zone for a week or two every year from 1975 to 1980 and then three to four times a year until 1988. I also acted as a medical director there one summer, when I took my family along with me. My wife and children still talk about that visit. The SLZH coordinated the visits of itinerant health care providers to the various communities. I visited most of these remote, isolated First Nations communities and provided necessary medical care. The nurses in charge decided who needed to be seen. During my visits, in my spare time, I made it a point also to see the school, community grocery store, and band council office and take an evening stroll around the town. I always tried to meet with the Chief and the members of the band council to learn about their needs. For our meals, we carried a food box provided by the SLZH, containing vegetables, bread, pasta and canned beans or meat. I used to take my own Indian spices and most evenings cooked curries for the nursing staff and myself, which made me the most sought-after consultant! Evening meals together bonded us and helped us debrief on daily events and release the stress of isolation. The nurses at times felt very isolated and depressed and particularly during the long and harsh winters suffered from cabin fever and were ready to quit. Recognizing this, I would request the SLZH director to extend my visit for a day or two.

I stopped visiting the Sioux Lookout in 1988 due to my increasing teaching and administrative commitments at the universities. However, in 1990, I founded the Visiting Lectureship Program on Native Health at the University of Toronto to provide a forum for Indigenous health experts to voice their lived experiences and observations, which could be useful to educate future health care professionals. This program lasted till my retirement in 2001.

My visits to the Sioux Lookout proved to be stressful for my wife. Flying to those remote areas in a small aircraft that either landed on a lake with a float in the summers or on skis on frozen lakes during harsh and unpredictable weather was quite risky. Every time I left home, I would make sure that my wife knew all the details about my will and financial affairs. Not only did she have to care for our two young sons but also constantly live with the fear of losing me. In 1978, while I was visiting a remote community during the winter, the weather took an extreme turn—radio communication between our main station and the clinic was unavailable. Somehow, a rumour spread that on my return flight the plane had crashed, and I was presumed dead. Our main outpost was almost ready to call my wife when radio communication came back, and I was confirmed alive.

For our travels to the northern communities, we were always provided with an "emergency bag" consisting of an insulated sleeping bag, some food, a whistle, and a small tent; we had already received survival courses in case of a plane crash. This apprehension about my risky sojourns did create some friction between my wife and me. But gradually she realized that this was my calling. My lasting regret is not having spent enough time with my family.

After my retirement from the university in 2001, I was invited to work as a primary care physician at Anishnawbe Health Toronto (AHT), a community health centre, by its Executive Director, Joe Hester, and so I transformed into a real doctor again! I soon realized how little I still knew about Indigenous communities. Joe Hester, a progressive thinker and a visionary, became my mentor. I got insight into Indigenous ways of dealing with health issues, which included the importance of Indigenous concepts of health and well-being and traditional healing practices. I worked side by side with traditional healers, and we complemented each other's knowledge and experiences.

Those fifteen years of postretirement were some of the most fulfilling of my life. During that period, I created the Aboriginal Cultural Safety Initiative in 2010, aimed at increasing the exposure of students and future health care practitioners to societal and health problems facing Indigenous individuals. This program was very successful and is currently progressing towards being permanently implemented in all health sciences curriculums at the college and university levels in Ontario.

In 1992 I was fortunate to be able to visit Indigenous communities abroad, namely the Aborigines of Australia and the Māori of New Zealand on a WHO fellowship. Initially I visited the Australian capital Canberra to study their government policies towards the Aborigines. From there I travelled to Darwin and several coastal communities in the northeast. There was a trip to Melville Island near Darwin and a visit to the Aborigine hospital in Darwin. Milikapiti was a settlement of the Tiwi people in Melville Island with a population over 500 people on a small plain. It was a coastal semitropical place with a lot of rain where the Tiwi could grow vegetables year-round. I visited their grocery store to find out the type and availability of food. To my amazement, I saw canned cucumber. I was struck at how dependent the settlers had made the local inhabitants—who did not even grow their own cucumber! On our flight back, I noticed that many inhabitants had lined up, moving towards a certain building. I found out that they were all going to the local tavern which opened for two hours a day, 4–6 p.m. Alcohol was allowed only once a day and was limited to two drinks per person. Back in Darwin I visited the hospital for Aborigines and was surprised to find most beds empty. Apparently, the patients did not like the hospital setting and preferred to be outdoor under the trees. Someone in Canberra had designed the hospital without knowing the needs of the Indigenous people, a similar situation to what happened in Canada.

In Auckland, New Zealand, I visited a government office where they did population projections. They had projected that by 2040 the Māori would make up 48.5 percent of the total population—if they did not change their immigration policy to allow non-white people to immigrate to New Zealand. From Auckland, I travelled to

Hamilton and visited one of their marae. As a WHO Fellow, I was greeted with their traditional ceremony, which was quite exhilarating. Following this, I met with their health council and later there was an elaborate lunch prepared for my wife and me. I was overall impressed by the Māori people. Back in 1840, they had signed the Treaty of Waitangi with the British Crown which included a clause for Māori representation in their government. By 1868 they already had their four members of parliament. Following my visit, with the help of a colleague, I wrote an article comparing the health status of Canadian First Nations People, the Aborigines of Australia, and the Māori of New Zealand. While all Indigenous people had suffered under colonial policies, the Māori had done better than both the Canadian and the Australian Indigenous people.

In 1999 I received a second WHO Fellowship, this time to visit Arizona and New Mexico and visit the Indigenous people there. This included a trip to Window Rock, the capital of Navajo Nation, where I met their president. I was most impressed with the progress the Navajo Nation had made in their infrastructure in education and job creation. I also visited several Indigenous communities south of Tucson where Pima Indians lived. Obesity and adult-onset diabetes were rampant in these communities. My visit to the community grocery stores revealed that they were stacked with sugar-loaded carbonated drinks. This being a hot country, they perspired a lot and were thirsty; to quench their thirst, they drank carbonated sweet drinks, leading them to urinate more which led them to drink more, the vicious cycle exacerbating obesity and diabetes. The community had realized this relationship and were about to ban sweetened carbonated drinks. In New Mexico, we visited several Indigenous communities called the Pueblos; many of them were situated on mountaintops. Our visit to the Santa Fe Indigenous pottery museum revealed how culturally advanced these people were at one time.

I realized that Britain as a colonial power had implemented similar policies when it came to Indigenous peoples across the globe; only the time of colonization and the density of the Indigenous peoples differed from place to place. The colonized suffered from loss of identity, culture, language, and belief systems. They have been dispossessed of land and livelihood, socially discriminated against, and faced racism—creating dependency and despondency.

As a South Asian who had spent the first twenty-six years of my life in India, I observed that India, though once colonized, probably suffered less because the country possessed written languages, established religious practices, and a larger population density that helped it to retain or regain identities much faster after Independence. Not having a written language, in my thinking, is one of the major risk factors of cultural genocide for colonized people. This understanding further clarified in my mind the devastating impact of colonization on the Indigenous people of Canada. It always warmed my heart when during some of my visits to the Indigenous communities in Australia, I was offered a job even without my asking. I had always respected Indigenous peoples' instincts to see through things, especially to see if outsiders' interests in them were genuine.

While there have been many reports on the Aboriginal situation in Canada, including the Royal Commission Report in 1997, the most influential one, which may transform Canada, is Justice Sinclair's report of 2015 on Truth and Reconciliation. It made ninety-four recommendations. While some of them have been acted upon, others have been delayed or not at all acted on. Meanwhile in 2019, the federal government had received the final report on Murdered and Missing Indigenous Women and Girls with 231 recommendations, which was accepted by the government without an action plan. If all this were not enough, to my shock and to the horror of many Canadians, there came reports of the discovery of mass unmarked graves of 215 Indigenous children on the grounds of a former residential school in Kamloops, British Columbia. Canadians from coast to coast were deeply affected. There is now increased resilience and a resurgence and reclamation of Indigenous identity and rights, bringing hope that their long-held demands for self-government will become a reality.

While presenting a paper on the prevalence of disability in the Indigenous communities in 1987, I was surprised by the attention this report garnered. These facts were already known to Indigenous communities and health care workers. Then it hit me—as a professor I was considered impartial and an authority, and I realized that my voice did count and could be instrumental in shaping public policies.

Historically, due to negotiated treaties, Indigenous communities have relied on the government for funding. For various reasons the government could not meet all funding demands, therefore in 2011, Joe Hester, Jacques Huot, and I set up the Anishnawbe Health Foundation to raise funds. I became one of the founding directors and still (2023) serve. I was a secretary-treasurer from 2016–19. Somehow over the years I had developed a knack for fundraising. I had realized that to raise funds, while stating facts and figures was necessary, to be effective one should be able to tell heart-wrenching stories from personal experiences, touching the hearts of donors; being a clinician, this was easy for me. I never hesitated to ask for money for a good cause, if I did not benefit personally.

In 1996, when I was working two half-days a week at the Anishnawbe Health Centre in Toronto as a primary care physician, a young, petite Aboriginal woman with chronic health problems came in. Afraid of men due to her past unpleasant experiences, she would not look up, so that all communication occurred through the accompanying nurse. I told her, "I am neither man nor woman, just a healer." Over time, she warmed up to me and called me Healer Shah. With the help of a traditional healer, the nurses, and I, this timid and shy woman blossomed into a community leader. She even came to one of my classes and addressed 250 medical students on doctor-patient relationships. We had helped her heal in mind, body, and spirit. I also learned about the "smudging ceremony"—a traditional Indigenous ritual in which sacred medicines such as cedar, sage, sweet grass or tobacco are lighted and burned in seashells to create smoke that is gently wafted by hand or an eagle feather to the person who is being smudged. The person inhales the smoke slowly. This is done to cleanse the soul of negative thoughts. I occasionally did this ceremony with my patients who needed spiritual healing. As many urban Indigenous Peoples had converted to Christianity and had therefore been forbidden from performing or partaking in all sorts of Indigenous ceremonies, this was their first experience with the smudging ceremony. We often laughed at the end, at the irony that I, a non-Indigenous person, was introducing them to their own ritual.

I was fortunate to find a very bright graduate student, David Buckridge, and a colleague, Brent Moloughney, who worked with me on the impact of spirituality on the health of the population. We recognized that spirituality is not synonymous with religiosity, even though over the course of history people have acquired spiritual teachings through religion. For the sake of research, we were able to tease out the three major mechanisms that influenced the health of spiritual individuals: being connected with a higher power (having faith), being less stressed (inner happiness), and having social connectedness. There has been much research done on the impact of religion on health and the impact of stress and social connectedness on health. We developed a mathematical model in 1997 to study the impact of spirituality on health and found that if Canadians were more spiritual (had regular attendance at the place of worship as a proxy measure), we could save 43,000 lives per year.

The study therefore justified the inclusion of spirituality in course curricula and medical practices. The findings received wide publicity in print, radio, and television media, and I was invited to be a keynote speaker in the first Canadian Conference on Spirituality and Health in Calgary in 1999. I am delighted that many medical schools in Canada and the US now teach spirituality and health as a part of their curriculum. However, public health as a field has lagged by not including spirituality in its programs.

What I've mentioned in the previous pages are just snapshots of times exciting and satisfying in the tumultuous life I have led. What did all these experiences teach me? That I cannot remain a bystander whenever I encounter social injustice and racism. I learned that silence can be violence. Since a segment of our population had no voice, as I saw it, I picked up the courage to speak up and provide its perspectives. As a physician, I must take care of a patient's physical ailments; but I should also attend to their mental, social, and spiritual well-being. I tried to promote traditional healing as part of health care for the Indigenous peoples and spiritual healing such as yoga and meditation for others. I learned that health care providers need empathy and compassion. I learned also that to make or alter public policies, policymakers need to know the cost of suffering, either in monetary costs or social costs. I remember talking to the president of the University of Toronto in 1976 about whether the university should commit itself to social responsibility. He strongly disagreed. In his view, the only responsibility professors have is to teach and create new knowledge through research, and then to publish their findings and let others using the new knowledge implement the required changes. I did not agree completely with him then, I do not agree with him now. Fortunately, over the years, the code of attitudes within the university has changed and the notion of "social responsibility" is no longer foreign.

3

A Personal Note

As I have said previously, several factors from my early life have helped me keep steadily on course. My upbringing in the Jain faith has helped me enormously. Jainism is one of the world's oldest religions, originating in India at least 2,500 years ago. The spiritual goal of Jainism is to become liberated from the endless cycle of rebirth and to achieve an all-knowing state called *moksha*. This can be attained by living a nonviolent life, or *ahimsa*, with as little negative impact on other life forms as possible (which concept we identify now as perfect harmony with our ecosystem). The traditions of Jainism were largely carried forward by a succession of twenty-four *tirthankaras*, or teachers, most notably Vardhamana Mahavira, the last of the tirthankaras and likely a contemporary of Gautama Buddha. Today, a sliver of India's population (0.4 percent) identifies itself as Jain, making it the smallest of the country's six major religious groups after Hinduism, Islam, Christianity, Sikhism, and Buddhism. Jains are vegetarians.

The teaching of nonviolence in that faith includes all forms of life in nature, it also instructs us not to injure anyone through words and thoughts. If knowingly or unknowingly one does hurt someone, one should ask for forgiveness. The other Jain teaching is to accept different viewpoints, which helps us to live in harmony with everything around us.

I would like to cite two events in my life which may shed some light on my belief. When I was about nine years old, I would go to our Jain temple daily and sought teachings from a Jain monk who stayed in our town for four months during the monsoon. I was of an impressionable age, and he thought I should learn by heart some Jain scriptures in their ancient Indian language, which was like Latin to me but these scriptures were recited daily by practicing Jains for atonement. During his stay I memorized a small part of a scripture. At the end of the monsoon season, it was customary to take a religious vow from the departing monk to live an austere life by giving up (sacrificing) something you love. In my case, he suggested that I give up rice and rice products till I had finished memorizing the scripture. I agreed. Once he left, I lost my interest in learning the text; however, true to my vow, I did not eat rice for the next eight years. For an Indian vegetarian in a Gujarati family, this was extremely difficult, but my family accommodated my diet. After eight years, when it became apparent that I would be leaving home to attend university, my father declared the riot act, telling me that unless I fulfilled my vow to learn the scripture by heart, he would not allow me to go. As a Jain, I also did not eat any root vegetables like potatoes, onions, and carrots, so my father was quite worried about how I would manage in a college dormitory. That summer I finally memorized the scripture and was able to recite it.

I would be remiss if I did not admit that I swayed again from my faith later in my life when I migrated to Canada. With all the difficulties associated with being a vegetarian earlier, I started consuming meat occasionally, particularly outside the home. Sudha never swayed from the faith and during our frequent visits to India, both our families were impressed at our sons remaining vegetarians. Once a year, Jains atone by fasting and asking for forgiveness of all living things in a communal ceremony. While Sudha, my younger son Rajiv and I observed this ritual, my older son Sunil was reluctant. I gave him a lecture about the virtue of this observance and the importance of keeping our cultural heritage. To appease me, he observed the ritual. A few days later, to my utter shame, he asked me why I was eating meat, which was against our religion and compelling him to practise our rituals? He asked, "Is faith only to be practised once a year?" And so I became a vegetarian once again.

Jainism has taught me that to be well and healthy one must harmonize four areas in one's life: physical, emotional, cognitive, and spiritual. By 1998 I began to understand the folly of the Western worldview of health (which had been inculcated in me), that is, the Cartesian approach. We separate mind and body and forget that spiritual belief plays an important role in keeping us going. The two are part of one. We talk about a heart-disease patient, forgetting that they are a person with other facets of life and not just heart disease. Slowly, I grasped the concept of holistic health and realized that we need to include spirituality as an important part of our public health care system.

I was also exposed to Gandhian nonviolence, treating all as equals without consideration of their caste or creed. (India always had discriminatory practice towards the lower [Dalit] castes; moreover, it has its own *Adivasis* or First Nations, which is an almost literal translation.) Gandhi was also an activist, always speaking out and fighting injustice, including British colonialism. His example guided me in my work against racism and my advocacy for marginalized people, including the Indigenous of Canada.

The *Gita* was another influence, when it says you should fight for the right cause whether you win or lose, without expecting any reward. My father's teachings on how to live a good and philosophical life also brought me inner peace during difficult times.

In 2000, Elder Lillian McGregor on behalf of the First Nations

House, Indigenous Student Services at the University of Toronto presented me the Eagle Feather for my work in promoting Indigenous issues at the University of Toronto. The Eagle Feather is a symbol of strength, wisdom and guidance; it connects the earth with the sky. Eagles are often seen to represent this connection. I was then required to learn seven Grandfather Teachings from Elder McGregor: Wisdom, Bravery, Honesty, Respect, Truth, Humility and Love. I also learned from her respect for Mother Earth, the importance of culture, language, and identity and the dehumanizing effect of racism and discrimination. It taught me what Indigenous peoples call "all our relations," meaning that we are all children of Mother Earth, though we may look different. To reduce inequality, we must appeal to people's spiritual beliefs.

An instance I'd like to touch upon now is from my high school days. In January 2001, I was visiting Mumbai and staying with my relatives. One day I received a phone call from Jaswant, my best friend from grade eight to eleven in high school and right up to our pre-medical years. We were almost inseparable. I had not seen him for almost forty years and had lost touch with him; all I knew about him was that he became a mathematics professor and had now retired and was living with his son in Surat. He wanted to visit me with his wife. According to Indian custom, his wife and he would be our guests, living with us. While I was ecstatic to see him after almost four decades, I was also a bit hesitant, as I did not wish to impose upon my hosts. Jaswant realized the reason for my discomfort, he assured me that it would be a very brief visit, and he would be returning that evening. He and his wife travelled 230 kilometres from Surat and arrived the next day. He had brought me a gift, which I declined—as part of our spiritual journey, my wife and I stopped accepting gifts when we both turned fifty-five—a part of our spiritual journey to reduce attachments to material things.

During our reminiscences he said that before he met me in grade eight, he had not been seriously interested in studies, all he cared about was sports. Excellent at volleyball, he was the team captain in school. His father had died when he was young, and a few years before I met him, his younger brother was murdered. With our friendship, he learned the importance of education, studied hard, got his master's in mathematics and became a professor. He gave me credit for his transformation and wanted to thank me for what he had achieved and wanted his wife to meet me. We were all extremely moved. We renewed our friendship and visited him in Surat whenever I visited India.

As mentioned earlier, I knew that with all my involvement outside the home, my family did suffer silently. One of the things that haunts me is the memory of not being able to formally celebrate my younger son Rajiv's graduation from medical school (1995), his specialty certification as an obstetrician and gynecologist (2001), followed by his attaining a master's degree in clinical epidemiology (2003) while he was still carrying out full-time practice. University graduation was expected in our family, but he had excelled far more, and I was oblivious to all his precious achievements. Once I realized my parental duty, I organized a surprise party for him, inviting his friends and colleagues. In my later years, I realized that when your life and work are done, all you have is your family.

I do not want to give the impression that all I did was work and there was no play. I enjoyed hosting dinner parties for our friends and family, and Sudha and I were known for our great parties. I enjoyed cooking as much as my work. I never needed a cookbook. This skill has served me well in my retirement. The other thing my wife and I enjoy is travelling around the world; we have been to all six continents including the Arctic. I write poetry in Gujarati and recite my poems at special occasions for my family and friends.

4

The Citizenship Examination and Indigenous History

I immigrated to Canada in 1965 and received my Canadian citizenship in 1970. At that time, as a Commonwealth citizen, all I needed to become a citizen was to take an oath in front of a citizenship judge. No examination was required. My wife, who came to Canada in 1966, did not promptly apply for her citizenship because of a reluctance to give up her Indian citizenship. In 1988, however, she decided to apply. Rules had changed by then. As per the new rules, one needed to appear and pass a citizenship test to be eligible to obtain Canadian citizenship. This test aims to evaluate whether applicants possess enough knowledge concerning Canadian history and the political system that the typical Canadian is expected to know. Information that could be included in the test might range from the names of provinces to the name of the first prime minister to the date of confederation.

The content of the citizenship test at the time was available in a guide that the Canadian government had assembled, a document that suddenly became ever present in our house. Out of curiosity, I skimmed through the guide, not expecting much new information. In the following pages, I have often used interchangeable terminology for Indigenous peoples using the terms "Native" or "Aboriginal";

it was the prevalent language in the 1990s when I carried out this work.

In the test booklet, I read the following about Indigenous peoples:

> The Indians and Inuit (also called Eskimos) lived in this country long before it was also known as Canada. They developed many languages and cultures. Their different ways of life developed in relation to the land and vegetation, wildlife and weather unique to different parts of the country. Corn, potatoes and tobacco were first cultivated by natives of America, and they invented the kayak, canoe and snowshoes.

By this point in my life, I had developed a deeper understanding of Canadian history and culture. Since my arrival on Canadian shores, I had learned about Canada as it was before the arrival of settlers, about the Indigenous peoples who had lived across the vast territory, and about their lives after the colonial powers took their lands from them through unfair treaties and forceful eviction. Because of this deeper understanding, I was quite taken aback by the sheer lack of information about those very Indigenous peoples. The guide did not mention anything about the treaties signed between the Crown and different tribes before and after confederation, and what obligations Canada has towards the people under those treaties. Treaties are signed between nations—obligations signed under the treaties are perpetual in nature. By signing them, Canada had accorded nationhoods to different Indigenous communities! All Canadians were "treaty people"!

I was distressed because new Canadians were becoming citizens without understanding or even any knowledge of Canada's past before its recent political history; most have no knowledge of the land's colonization and the unfair and even brutal treatment of Indigenous peoples; they have no knowledge, and most don't care about the recent status of the Indigenous.

I viewed the lack of information concerning Indigenous history in the citizenship-test guide as either a slight or oversight regarding the Indigenous population and their ancestors. I believed that it was important for new Canadians to have a fuller and accurate understanding of their adopted country's history and culture. Many of them came from recently colonized places themselves and so would have natural empathy for the Indigenous people. Of course, ironically, most white Canadians born here have no understanding or care either about the country's real history. Hopefully that will change.

Appalled by the lack of adequate information about the history of the Indigenous peoples in the citizenship guide, I began to devise a strategy that would allow me to draw attention to this unfortunate error repeating itself after 125 years of confederation. At the time, I had developed a large network within the public service sector and decided that using my familiarity with these contacts would help me make the content of the citizenship guide a pressing issue for the Department of Multiculturalism and Citizenship.

Since this issue was one that the Canadian government was directly responsible for, I believed that if I gained support from credible groups and persons for my cause, it would affect necessary changes in the Citizenship Guide and examination. Before my journey into this unknown territory, I also consulted the Honourable Justice Rosalie Abella, who was later appointed to the Supreme Court of Canada in 2004. A sympathetic listener, she confirmed that this issue was indeed in the political realm, granting me a sense of confidence.

At the heart of my campaign for greater inclusion of Indigenous history was a personal letter campaign. In 1991, I sent more than twenty-five letters to individuals and organizations who could further my cause through May and June. These entities spanned

Canada and included Toronto mayor Art Eggleton's office, the Canadian Public Health Association, and the Ontario Public Health Association (both of which I was a member of), the archbishop of the Anglican Church of Canada, moderator of the United Church of Canada, the National Catholic Bishops' Assembly, the Assembly of First Nations, the Union of Ontario Indians, and the Native Council of Canada.

The letter explained the nature of the issue, how we could resolve the lack of material in the citizenship guide and the contact information for the individual government officials who had the authority to effect change directly. The following excerpt catches the spirit of the letter I wrote:

> I have a specific proposal that I would like to bring to the attention of your organization. The proposal deals with social justice by increasing the understanding of Aboriginal people in a historical context, thus creating racial harmony in Canada and nation-building . . .

> Many of our native people are the poorest of the poor in this country. Their health status is a national disgrace. Many of these could be related to colonization, the imposition of an alien culture and post-colonial administrative policies. This could be understood only if one studies this in the historical context. As indicated above, many of the new citizens of this country have very little background knowledge of history.

> In recent years, with the increased emphasis by the Indigenous Peoples on self-determination and land claims settlements, it has become imperative that the non-native group, including new Canadians, understand the struggle of the natives for their rights. This would help the building of Canada in a just and fair manner.

Hence I would like the Canadian Government to initiate a program that would consider the following: all the new immigrants, particularly the prospective candidates for citizenship in Canada, receive education about the Indigenous Peoples (Indians and Inuit) in terms of their lifestyles before the colonization, the treaties signed by the British Crown with the Aboriginal people during colonization and after the confederation, major obligations under the treaties that the Canadian population has towards natives, and how we have met those obligations over the past 124 years. There should be questions on Aboriginal people in the citizenship examination; otherwise, people tend to ignore the historical material as not relevant.

I request that your organization endorse the proposal and write to the following government ministers, raising the above issue and asking them to implement a program that would consider the principles outlined above.

In summary, this is a modest proposal, which, if implemented, could go a long way in instituting social justice and racial harmony, and building Canada for the next century for all its people and not just a select few.

While a few agencies and persons did not endorse my proposed reform, I received several positive responses to my requests from groups like the Canadian Public Health Association, the City of Toronto, and the Ontario Social Development Council. Particularly, the Canadian Public Health Association was active in furthering my letter-writing campaign, sending letters endorsing my reform proposal to the Citizenship Judges, the Department of Multiculturalism and Citizenship, and the Minister of Employment and Immigration. The City Council of Toronto voted to create amendments that would support accurate and detailed Aboriginal history and openly endorsed my cause.

The responses to my letters to the parties within the government generally followed a similar pattern. They outlined some of their initiatives to increase Aboriginal information access and informed me that it would be better for me to discuss the issue with the Minister of Multiculturalism and Citizenship. In the process, I met a staff member in the federal Department of Secretary of State, Charles (I deeply regret that I have forgotten his last name), a Métis man who understood what I was trying to accomplish. He became an internal agent of change within the government, and I am extremely grateful for his contributions to the effort.

In August 1991, I received a response from the Minister of Multiculturalism and Citizenship. It informed me that the minister was very appreciative of my comments and "desire to increase racial harmony in Canada."

I also received a letter from Senior Citizenship Judge, Hon Elizabeth Willcock, assuring me that " . . . the Citizenship Judge would be most supportive of including this important aspect of Canada's heritage as part of the Citizenship hearing and, Dr Shah, you will have my complete cooperation in this important endeavour." The deputy minister of the Citizenship Department to Ottawa invited me for a meeting where I was informed that the Citizenship Registration and Promotion Branch of the department reviewed the content of the educational materials for citizenship applicants. I was assured that they would take my comments and proposed reforms into account in their new citizenship document.

At the time, I was unsure whether my words and actions had truly effected change—was I being placated for the time being? Over time I learned that the only way to truly effect change is to sustain one's efforts until one sees the change. Consistent questioning and correspondence allow one to become immersed in the process of change gradually.

In 1994, the new and improved Citizenship Test Guide was released to the public. I received a phone call from Charles to inform me about the results of my efforts and congratulate me. Unfortunately, I was absent from my office that day. When he later phoned me at home, I was out of town, and he ended up conveying the message to my wife Sudha, profusely thanking me for my efforts on behalf of Aboriginal peoples. He praised me in such an enthusiastic manner that when I recount this experience, I often joke that since that day I could do no wrong in Sudha's eyes! This phone call also helped Sudha to understand my long periods of absence and to forgive my sometimes neglecting my own family. Now, I started hearing her boasting about my work!

I was delighted to note the appearance of a lengthy section concerning Aboriginal history in Canada and the inclusion of questions in the citizenship examination concerning Aboriginal people. The updated section made distinctions between the groups of Aboriginal peoples and explained the treaties they signed. The following is an excerpt from the updated section in 1994:

> The ancestors of Aboriginal peoples are believed to have migrated from Asia many thousands of years ago. They were well established here long before explorers from Europe first came to North America. Diverse, vibrant First Nations cultures were rooted in religious beliefs about their relationship to the Creator, the natural environment and each other.
>
> Aboriginal and treaty rights are in the Canadian Constitution. Territorial rights were first guaranteed through the Royal Proclamation of 1763 by King George III and established the basis for negotiating treaties

with the newcomers—treaties that were not always fully respected.

From the 1800s until the 1980s, the federal government placed many Aboriginal children in residential schools to educate and assimilate them into mainstream Canadian culture. The schools were poorly funded and inflicted hardship on the students; some were physically abused. Aboriginal languages and cultural practices were mostly prohibited. In 2008, Ottawa formally apologized to the former students.

Today, the term Aboriginal peoples refer to three distinct groups: Indian refers to all Aboriginal people who are not Inuit or Métis. In the 1970s, the term First Nations began to be used. Today, about half of First Nations people live on reserve land in about 600 communities while the other half live off-reserve, mainly in urban centres.

The Inuit, which means "the people" in the Inuktitut language, live in small, scattered communities across the Arctic. Their knowledge of the land, sea and wildlife enabled them to adapt to one of the harshest environments on earth.

The Métis are a distinct people of mixed Aboriginal and European ancestry, the majority of whom live in the Prairie Provinces. They come from both French- and English-speaking backgrounds and speak their own dialect, Michif.

About 65 percent of the Aboriginal people are First Nations, while 30 percent are Métis and 4 percent Inuit. (Government Canada 2012)

Subsequent guides in 1999, 2004, 2010 and 2017 have

maintained and augmented these changes. *Statistics Canada* reports that approximately 215,000 immigrants have received their Canadian citizenship every year since 1994, resulting in almost six million immigrants (at the time of writing) benefiting from the change in test content in the past twenty-six years. It seemed that change had indeed happened, and I believe it has helped Canada become a more informed society, increase racial harmony, and build an inclusive nation. This action was in keeping with the spirit of the 93rd Recommendation of the Truth and Reconciliation Commission of Canada, some twenty years ago, which states (Truth and Reconciliation Commission 2015):

> We call upon the federal government, in collaboration with the national Aboriginal organizations, to revise the information kit for newcomers to Canada and its citizen-ship test to reflect a more inclusive history of the diverse Aboriginal peoples of Canada, including information about the Treaties and history of residential schools.

5

Combating Unconscious Bias

Many people, including immigrants and the educated in our society, have an unconscious (or conscious) bias and stereotypical negative image of Indigenous peoples. I witnessed this in my patients, who came to me upset or crying because of mistreatment by non-Aboriginal health care workers. I recall a sixty-five-year-old Indigenous woman with early symptoms of stroke, who was labeled "drunken" in two emergency rooms in Toronto and discharged. Finally, she went to a third emergency room with a white friend and received treatment. But she now suffers residual effects of that stroke.

In another instance, a disabled man, who visited the emergency room at one of Toronto's hospitals, stuck this note to the entrance of our clinic door:

> Dr Shah, I have been assaulted by hospital security. They are charging (me) with assault on the 250+ lbs guard, resisting arrest and trespassing. I am afraid to go home because the cops are waiting to arrest me. Their Dr—did not even get a chance to see me. Help. 8:15 a.m. I have waited since 7:10 a.m. Too cold. Going home.

This patient of mine had multiple health problems, used a walker to move and probably weighed no more than 125 pounds. This was his emergency-room encounter! It seemed at times it was a crime to be Indigenous in Canada.

Yet another example vivid in my mind is of an Aboriginal woman in her mid-fifties, with whom I thought I had a great patient-physician relationship. She came frequently with physical complaints that I could not diagnose. Finally, after two years, she revealed to me that she had been sexually abused from age seven to ten in a residential school. I was the first person she was telling this.

Often, we are not conscious of our biases; they are triggered automatically by our brain making quick judgments and assessments of people and situations, influenced by our background, cultural environment, and personal experiences. Such implicit or unconscious bias among health and social service providers plays a crucial role in health care disparities just as it plays a role elsewhere in society, for example how children are treated in schools. It was shocking for me to note how widespread this unconscious bias was in undergraduate students towards Indigenous peoples. It was an uphill task to initiate an educational program to combat their stereotypical views. In the following pages, I have also used "Native" and "Aboriginal" for Indigenous peoples—they were the prevalent terms used in the 1990s.

Indigenous Health Education at the University of Toronto in the 1990s

In 1982, I became very cognizant of the health issues of Indigenous peoples and the social and political determinants of their health. The quality of Indigenous health was in a desperate state, and as usual too few people except the Indigenous themselves were actively attempting to ameliorate this sad situation. To improve the quality of life of the Indigenous peoples, public awareness about their problems needed to increase drastically. So was the need to train future health care providers in Aboriginal health issues so that they would provide culturally sensitive health care to the Indigenous in their future practices. To do this, centres of higher learning, such as the University of Toronto, had to become leaders by incorporating Aboriginal health issues in their health sciences curricula, providing a forum for public advocacy, and inspiring others to devote their energies to supporting Aboriginal peoples. But as I looked around me at the University of Toronto, especially my own Public Health Sciences department (now known as the Dalla Lana School of Public Health), I realized that barely any efforts were being made to investigate Aboriginal peoples' difficulties or create Aboriginal support movements that others could rally around. I was disappointed, but not discouraged, and began to dream about the possibility of a permanent position for an Indigenous professor within Public Health Sciences who would be devoted to Aboriginal health.

In 1981, I wrote to the dean of medicine and subsequently to the two deans who came after him, urging them to create such a professorship. In my letters, I focused on conveying the social changes this move could inspire within the university and in Canada. Woefully, the deans did not respond and my attempts to discuss the topic with them in person were always thwarted. I began to realize that I would have to initiate such a post through public support.

As a professor in the Public Health Sciences faculty and a researcher in Aboriginal health, I would often get invited by different health and social sciences faculties at the University to give a one or two-hour classroom lecture on Aboriginal health. These lectures were given in departments of pharmacy, nursing, dentistry, and social work, drawing approximately 100 to 150 students to each lecture.

I made it a point to begin my talks with a simple activity that I felt gauged the level of understanding that students had about

Aboriginal peoples. I would ask, "What adjectives come to your mind when you think about Aboriginal peoples?" They were given the freedom to say whatever came to mind, no matter how that might be construed. Before they answered, I would usually turn my back to them, facing the blackboard, to afford them a greater sense of personal safety. Students were generally honest in their verbal responses, and I would write down most of their thoughts on the blackboard. Following that, I would undertake the activity again but for a different ethnic group such as Chinese, German, or French people. After writing down their responses, I would turn back towards my class and ask those who actually knew an Aboriginal person to raise their hands. Generally, about ten hands would be in the air at this stage. I would then ask how many students in the class had been to lunch with an Aboriginal person they knew. At this point, four to five of the hands would drop. Finally, I asked my audience if any of them had been to an Aboriginal person's house. Almost without fail, there would be no hands in the air. At this point, I would review their statements on the blackboard with them. Generally, almost 80 percent of their responses about the Aboriginal people were stereotypically negative, in stark contrast with their thoughts about the other ethnic groups, where almost 80 percent of the responses were positive.

I knew that the students in my class were not necessarily racist, and they could see the error in their assumptions at this point. To attempt to understand how such a bright group of people could succumb to such crude perspectives about an entire race, I would ask them how they accounted for the negative Aboriginal stereotypes. In the students' eyes, the largest culprit was the media, which portrayed negative images of Aboriginal peoples. While I could understand this perception, I was still constantly taken aback and would always remind them that the purpose of higher education was the development of critical thinking—I refused to let them off the hook because I knew they had the tools to combat the negativity of the media.

As I gave more and more lectures, the constant repetition of the same beliefs about Aboriginal peoples bothered me. I started to discover the extent of the lack of education about the Aboriginal peoples in higher learning. There was probably no education about Aboriginal peoples in primary or secondary school either. That's when an idea came to me—having some forum wherein I could bring Aboriginal peoples to the university campus to tell their own stories. I felt that if they told their stories and spoke about their lived experiences themselves instead of non-Aboriginal experts like me, it would have a bigger impact on listeners.

It was 1990 and Canada was going through a recession. The funding needed for such a forum was not available from the university, my own department, or nonprofit voluntary organizations. Canadian granting agencies did not provide for such annual forums. So to acquire the funds necessary for this advocacy endeavour, I began to approach several agencies and foundations, such as departments of federal and provincial governments dealing with Indigenous affairs, The Physicians' Services Incorporated Foundation, The Hospital for Sick Children Foundation asking for a small contribution from each, promising that I would not take their funds unless I was able to secure the required amounts for the next five years, which was pegged at $25,000. Many of my colleagues had doubts about my ability to raise such funds. By gathering donations from various groups (nowadays, we call it crowdsourcing), I secured funding for the forum of my dreams. I named it the Visiting Lectureship on Native Health (at that time, the word Indigenous was not in currency).

As mentioned earlier, in the late 1980s, the First Nations

People's health status was discouraging. Almost sixty percent of the Aboriginal population resided in urban settings; a large number were homeless. On the reserves the living conditions were shocking. Most houses were crowded and lacked sewage facilities and potable water. The unemployment rate in many communities was as high as 85 percent. The residential-school system, the "sixties scoop" where Indigenous children were removed from their families and placed or adopted in non-Indigenous families, discrimination, low education levels, insensitive health and social services, and lack of support networks all contributed to high levels of physical and mental illness. However, now many articulate Aboriginal individuals such as Phil Fontaine, Ovide Mercerdi, and Georges Erasmus had stepped forward, calling for change.

In summer of 1990 I announced the Visiting Lectureship Program on Native Health at the University of Toronto in several student newspapers, in personal letters to members of different faculties, and to several teaching hospitals. The first lecture was scheduled for October 1990. As I started advertising the program across the university, I received a phone call from the provost's office to tell me that I had not sought the necessary approval for a lectureship program. The insistence to follow the process prevailed, despite my appeal and candid admission that I had been unaware of the permissions required. It seemed as if all the great momentum the program had captured was about to dissipate due to this formality. Fortunately, a sudden provincial election had just been called and, to everybody's surprise, the provincial New Democratic Party (NDP) under the leadership of Hon Bob Rae won. Two months before the election was called, at the request of Mr Rae, I met him in his office and he asked if I would be willing to review some position papers their party was developing related to the health of vulnerable populations, to which I said yes. I was also well acquainted with Mr Rae's passion for Indigenous peoples' right to self-determination and one of the best papers written by him on the subject, *First One to Come and the Last to Be Served*. After the election, I invited Premier Rae to be the inaugural speaker in the program since he had been heavily involved in promoting Aboriginal issues in the past. He was the most suitable person to invite. Just when I had given up hope, the new premier's office called me to say that he had accepted my invitation. It would be his first public function as the premier of Ontario. Following this marvellous news, I called the provost's office to inform them about this development. There was now a sudden change in the provost's stance. His office informed me promptly that somebody had made a mistake—apparently, they had believed I was initiating a visiting professorship, not a visiting lectureship. I was permitted to continue with my planning.

This was the beginning of the eleven-year program. Every year in the fall term, three weeks were dedicated to Aboriginal experts discussing Aboriginal health issues and how to reshape the health care system so that it was culturally safe and inclusive of their concept of health and traditional healing practices. I led a planning committee composed of faculty members and students across the university, and members from the teaching hospital, Ontario Medical Association, City of Toronto Public Health Department, and the Anishnawbe Health Toronto, who were both Aboriginal and non-Aboriginal people. The committee decided the focus of the program each year and whom to invite to speak each week. The speakers came from across Canada, the only requirement being that they be Aboriginal and knowledgeable in their subject.

During our third year I ran into a quandary. The committee invited a certain Aboriginal speaker when one of its Aboriginal members happened to be absent. When he learned about the choice made in his absence, he vehemently objected. Apparently, the invited individual had a tarnished image in some Indigenous communities. By this time, I had already sent the invitation and I did not know how to rescind it. After much thinking, I consulted three Indigenous elders and sought their guidance. They unanimously agreed that I should withdraw my invitation. In my culture we believe that once you invite someone, you should not uninvite them. I had to do a great deal of soul-searching, after which I called the individual and explained the situation, including the advice from the elders, apologized profusely, and withdrew my invitation. Fortunately for me, the person was very considerate! This incident made me understand the true meaning of community engagement and empowerment.

The Aboriginal lecturers put together a two-hour presentation. They gave a lecture, seminar or workshop concerning Aboriginal health in several disciplines such as medicine, pharmacy, social work, nursing, anthropology, law, and teaching hospitals. These presentations were designed to be as accessible as possible for faculty, students, and staff members. The lecture would be part of a formal course and the students would be examined. After their presentations, the Aboriginal experts were available for consultation. I also shared the speakers with other university departments in the area, York University, Toronto Metropolitan (then Ryerson) University, and McMaster University, as well as the Canadian Memorial Chiropractic College, the Canadian Naturopathic College, and a few of the local high schools. As part of their commitment to the program, the speakers pledged to participate in a forum for public debate on Aboriginal health for a university-wide audience, and for a public audience at Toronto City Hall, which was held in the City's Council Chamber followed by a reception hosted by the mayor.

An Indigenous artist Ken Syrette was commissioned to develop the following logo for the program.

It is based on the Indigenous concept of holistic health called "medicine wheel," which comprises a circle; within it, the upper hand represents an Indigenous person who is imparting knowledge to a non-Indigenous person; the four feathers symbolize four races that are moving in harmony to enhance the health of Indigenous Peoples.

Each year the lectureship revolved around a specific Aboriginal health theme, and the program started with an inaugural public lecture. The keynote speakers were prominent Indigenous leaders. It was well publicized, with invitations to high-ranking officials from the teaching hospitals, public health departments, ministries of health, community leaders, activists, and the public. From within my university, the chancellor, members of the Governing Council, the president, provost, deans and chairs of various faculties attended the inaugural lecture. These events had a powerful impact. In one of the inaugural lectures, Phil Fontaine, a well-known Indigenous leader, vividly described his experiences in the residential school, including of him being sexually abused. It was an emotional moment throughout the hall. Another time a woman who identified herself as a nurse came to me after the lecture and thanked me, saying that she had hidden her Indigenous identity so far, but now felt proud of being Indigenous.

The first week of lectureship involved providing historical background, including the impact of colonization on Aboriginal people relevant to the topic chosen. The second week examined health and social issues as they existed now in Aboriginal communities. The third week focused on future solutions to these problems. The themes for the eleven years of the lectureship are as follows.

Table I: Themes of the Lectureship Series

Year	Theme
1990	Perspectives in Native Health
1991	Perspectives on Native Family Violence
1992	Perspectives on Urban Native Health: Life in the City
1993	Perspecitves on Native Community Healing and Substance Abuse
1994	Perspectives on Native Mental Health and Healing
1995	Perspectives on Aboriginal Women and Health
1996	Perspectives on Aboriginal Nutrition and Health
1997	Report of the Royal Commission on Aboriginal Peoples: Perspective on Health
1998	Traditional Healing Practices: Bridging the Gap
1999	Healthy Children: Healthy Nations
2000	Different Nations: Different Issues

Nearly 15,000 people attended the lecture series over the course of its run through eleven years. Much to my delight, the Visiting Lectureship Series and the health issues discussed received widespread media exposure too, with the Women's TV Network producing a one-hour program broadcast across the country in 1995. As the program became popular, donations kept pouring in; no longer did I need to go on my knees seeking for funds. I established a trust account to enhance Indigenous education. By 2000, I had already accumulated around $400,000.

Today, as I go down memory lane, it gives me immense satisfaction and happiness to realize that I was part of this historic development. Even decades after the commencement of this program, I can still recall the genuine feeling of satisfaction that was created.

The program celebrated its tenth anniversary in 1999; it was at this celebration that I was honoured with the Eagle Feather, as I have mentioned previously. The Minister of Health, Elizabeth Witmer, presented a $100,000 check to me to establish an Endowed Professorship for Aboriginal Health and Wellbeing in the Department of Public Health Sciences at the University of Toronto. As mentioned above, I had already collected $400,000 in our trust account, and with the health ministry's contribution, my total funds rose to $500,000.

At this point, I was also raising the issue with the University of Toronto for lack of visible minorities among the faculty. This had led to a meeting with the Provost Adel Sedra, at the end which I brought up an issue not related to our meeting. I told him one of my unfulfilled dreams before my retirement was to establish an endowed professorship in Aboriginal health. I had already single-handedly collected $500,000 and asked whether the University of Toronto would be kind enough to match it so that we could have an Endowed Professorship. As I had already cornered him on the university's lack of visible minority faculty, perhaps to appease me he right away promised to match the fund, making it a one-million dollar endowment. Some twenty years later in a function investing the new President Vivek Goel (my former student and colleague) at the University of Waterloo, I realized I had been wrong in my previous assumption. Professor Sedra came over to me and said he had really appreciated the Indigenous lectureship program and my work with diversifying the faculty membership and thanked me. I realized then that he was a silent angel supporting my work from within the university.

While Dean David Naylor and my chair Harvey Skinner of the Public Health Science department were extremely happy with my accomplishment, they suggested that I should have asked for more money from the university. They wanted to have an endowed chair, which required at that time an endowment fund of two million: one million from fundraising and a matching grant of one million from the university. The dean, with the help of a fundraiser and myself, was able to attract the remaining $500,000 from the TransCanada Pipeline. Thus, a two-million dollar fund was established for the TransCanada Pipelines Chair in Indigenous Health and Wellbeing to support an ongoing position for an Indigenous scholar. This was the first of its kind in Canada. Dr Jeff Reading, an Aboriginal scholar, became the first Endowed Chair of Indigenous Health & Wellbeing when he was hired in September 2000.

The Visiting Lectureship program was just the beginning to many progressive ideas that were executed over time. In the past twenty years, the University of Toronto has made tremendous progress in establishing many educational initiatives in Indigenous issues, including establishing the Waakebiness-Bryce Institute of Indigenous Health, a masters program in Indigenous Public Health, and developing special support services for Indigenous students, including scholarships. These new initiatives will help future generations of students be more sensitive to Aboriginal issues, create informed and caring citizens, and hopefully remove the prevalent "unconscious bias."

6

Indigenous Cultural Safety in Ontario's Colleges and Universities

After my retirement, I expected that the annual Visiting Lectureship Program would continue, but this did not happen, and it lapsed. I was upset because I had put in so much energy into building it. It felt like I had lost a part of myself. Over the next three years, I was flooded with enquiries from inside and outside the university about the Program—it's schedule, its topics, and so on. I tried, directly and indirectly, to influence the new chair to continue the program but to no avail. And I did not get a reason for the discontinuation. Finally, I came around to accepting that this was certainly not his priority, and that I needed to move on.

No more than two weeks into my retirement, I was invited to work as a primary care physician at Anishnawbe Health Toronto, a community health centre exclusively serving the urban Indigenous people in Toronto. Moreover, I received frequent invitations to lecture on Indigenous health and wellbeing by several faculties at universities acquainted with me through the Visiting Lectureship Program. With the shifting health care paradigm, health care providers understood the importance of culturally safe health care on health outcomes. The concept of culturally safe health care finally started emerging.

The Need for Cultural Safety

Before defining what culturally safe health care is, it is important to understand why such care is needed. Ontario has the highest number of Indigenous people in Canada. In 2016, 22.4 percent of people of Indigenous ancestry lived in Ontario. Almost 78 percent of Indigenous people reside in off-reserve (rural, non-reserve, and urban) communities. Whether they reside in First Nations communities or off-reserve, Indigenous people's health status is significantly lower than that of the general population in Ontario and Canada. The Indigenous population has experienced culturally insensitive health care and their members have met with subtle and overt racism. As recently as 2016, Brian Sinclair, an Aboriginal man in a wheelchair, died in the emergency room of Winnipeg Health Sciences Centre after waiting for thirty-four hours without anyone attending to him;[1] in 2020, Joyce Echaquan, a thirty-seven-year-old woman died in a Quebec hospital while she was requesting for help and being mocked by a nurse; all this was recorded live on her FaceTime.[2] The following quote by the Health Council of Canada provides a fundamental insight into the issues encountered by Indigenous people in the health care system:[3]

> It is well documented that many underlying factors negatively affect Indigenous people's health in Canada, including poverty and the intergenerational effects of colonization and residential schools. But one barrier to good health lies squarely in the lap of the health care system itself. Many Indigenous people don't trust—and therefore don't use—mainstream health care services because they

1 https://www.cbc.ca/news/canada/manitoba/roots-of-racism-in-winnipeg-revealed-in-brian-sinclair-inquest-1.2873729
2 https://en.wikipedia.org/wiki/Death_of_Joyce_Echaquan
3 https://publications.gc.ca/site/eng/9.698021/publication.html

don't feel safe from stereotyping and racism, and because the Western approach to health care can feel alienating and intimidating.

Irihapeti Ramsden, a Māori nurse of New Zealand, first introduced the concept of cultural safety in 1990. Her description of the term explained that cultural safety moves beyond cultural sensitivity and cultural competence (i.e., knowing the culture of "the other"). It analyses power imbalances in society and political ideals of self-determination and decolonization.

Our understanding of the influence of culture on health has evolved over the past five decades, resulting in chronological approaches and terminology adopted in the provision of health care such as i) cultural awareness, that is, one must realize that other cultures are distinct and often do not share many external similarities—thus the acknowledgement of differences between cultures becomes important; ii) cultural sensitivity, that is, understanding that in every culture there are some intrinsic values perhaps unique to it; iii) cultural competency, that is, the ability and knowledge to understand and appreciate cultural differences and similarities and to act accordingly; iv) cultural safety, that is, the provider or carer must reflect on all aspects of a patient's life, including life experiences and historical injustices suffered by their community. This reflection will lead to better understanding of the client and empathy towards them. This is a transitional stage, and when the client or patient perceives the empathy, the patient feels safe and enters a trust relationship with the carer. The carer also becomes an advocate for the patient and his or her communities.

Fulcher defined cultural safety as "that state of being in which the (individual) knows emotionally that her/his personal wellbeing, as well as social and cultural frames of reference, are acknowledged—even if not fully understood. Furthermore, she/he is given active reason to feel hopeful that her/his needs and those of her/his family members and kin will be accorded dignity and respect."

Even though I was a frontline worker and an academician, it took me a long time to understand the concept of cultural safety as explained by sociologists. A chance encounter with a fifty-five-year-old unemployed Indigenous patient with a minor medical problem helped me to understand its true meaning. I routinely checked new Indigenous patients' blood glucose levels since they were at a high risk for diabetes. I found his blood sugar very high. He was unaware of it. I prescribed medicines to treat his diabetes, ordered blood tests, and asked him to return for a follow-up in two weeks.

He returned after almost five months. I was upset and began to lecture (an old habit, thanks to being a professor) him on the importance of follow-up visits and adherence to his treatment plan for diabetes. After about two minutes of surviving my lecture, he stopped me and asked me to look at a piece of paper he had pulled out from his wallet. I grudgingly took the paper and found it to be his welfare payment statement. The statement showed that he was receiving $525 in monthly payment of which $325 was directly deposited for rent in his landlord's bank account. That's when I realized he would have been left with only $200 for food, transportation, clothing, telephone, and toiletries for the entire month. This worked out to be less than $7 a day! If he were to come for a follow-up visit, it would cost $6 for his round trip by bus, leaving him with $1 for that day! In a similar situation, would I see my doctor? Or would I eat instead? I needed to "walk in his shoes" to understand the gravity of his situation. I felt a deep pang of guilt.

I should have enquired about his social circumstances and been more reflective before giving him a scolding. To regain his trust and build a therapeutic relationship, I needed to have empathy. I should have understood his life situation and not been so judgemental.

When he perceives a listener in me, he will trust me. This is what cultural safety means in a real-life situation. And it took an embarrassing incident to make me understand the true meaning of the term! At the time of the incident, I was overcome by anger, shame, and multiple other feelings. But as is the case with many things in life, it is only later that one can connect the dots and realize that everything that happens, has a reason behind it. That meeting with the patient took me on a path that opened doors into several minds, a path I am lucky to have walked through.

As previously mentioned, after the conclusion of the Visiting Lectureship Program, after my so-called retirement, I continued to be invited to speak about Indigenous health and wellbeing at various forums in the Greater Toronto area. Over time, I began to note that the steady stream of invitations to lecture did not slow down. During this period, I was employed full-time to provide primary care at AHT. I was no longer a professor who lectured or conducted research, generating new knowledge. Fortunately, AHT's executive director Joe Hester knew me well, granted me half a day per week to research or promote issues related to Indigenous health.

There was a surge in demand for education about Indigenous people in postsecondary institutions and a shortage of Indigenous teachers, and I saw great prospects for developing an innovative method to deliver Indigenous health education in those institutions. However, before I could hope to initiate any efforts in this direction, I needed to carry out an environmental scan of postsecondary education in Ontario. This would provide me with the quantitative and qualitative evidence necessary to attract funding and public support for any planned program. As I had done before, I sent a web-based questionnaire via email to all health sciences program directors of Ontario colleges and universities, asking about their curriculum content on Indigenous health and how educators disseminated it.

Using a document prepared by the Indigenous Physicians Association of Canada and the Association of Faculties of Medicine of Canada titled, "First Nations, Inuit, Métis Health Core Competencies: A Curriculum Framework for Undergraduate Medical Education," survey questions were designed to ask program directors who had responded positively that they had indeed included Indigenous content in their courses, about the extent to which these core competencies were addressed in their curricula. I sent the questionnaire to a total of twenty-five colleges and forty university health science programs and got a response rate of about fifty percent, which we deemed satisfactory.

Other than nursing programs and a few personal care support programs, the Indigenous content in college curricula was nonexistent. In contrast, two-thirds of the university programs dealt with some aspect of Indigenous core competencies. The First Nations, Inuit, Métis Health Core Competencies document had stipulated that a competent Indigenous preceptor should teach the core competencies such as the impact of colonization and residential schools on the health of Indigenous people, Indigenous concepts of health and healing, traditional healing practices, living conditions on reserves, and the inaccessibility of health and social services. Since many colleges and universities would not have such an Indigenous expert available, I asked the respondents if they would consider including such an individual in their course if available on a session basis. The majority (81.8 percent) of college respondents indicated yes, and the remaining 18.2 percent said maybe. When we asked the same question to the university respondents, the majority (71.4 percent) also indicated yes, while 19.0 percent said maybe.

While many programs would have liked to expand to include Indigenous content, they cited specific deterrents in their comments, most notably a lack of time to teach any more courses, a lack of Indigenous faculty on their staff, and the misconception that their courses in cultural sensitivity in general would be adequate. They believed that Indigenous groups were similar enough to other cultural groups.

However, the document referenced above addressed quite eloquently the need for a stand-alone course on Indigenous cultural safety. The task force writes:

> Health disparities between First Nations, Inuit and Métis peoples and the general Canadian population continue to exist. Canada's history of colonization of First Nations, Inuit, and Métis peoples with its resulting racism, discrimination, and marginalization continues to affect many communities' health and wellbeing. As the First Peoples of Canada, these communities are diverse in their languages, beliefs, histories and health practices. And while varied languages, histories and health practices may also be true of cultural groups who have immigrated to Canada, First Nations, Inuit, and Métis peoples are not a cultural group to Canada, but rather distinct constitutionally recognized peoples with Indigenous and treaty rights.

The task force recommended that Colleges Ontario and the Council of Ontario Universities should have faculty development seminars and programs that concern Indigenous culture.

Development of the Program

The environmental scan very clearly indicated the lack of Indigenous education in the existing health sciences. This led to the birth of the Aboriginal Cultural Safety Initiative (ACSI), which strived to provide accessible knowledge from trained Indigenous volunteer instructors to university and college students enrolled in health science courses.

At that time, over 47,000 students were enrolled in the health sciences program in colleges and universities across Ontario.

I was extremely fortunate to receive a three-year grant from the Trillium Foundation for this initiative, along with additional supplemental funding from the Ontario Ministry of Training, Colleges, and Universities. This was an added responsibility for me; however, I was able to hire a part-time doctoral student Allison Reeves to assist me. Without her fantastic help, I think I would have drowned in work! The overarching goal of ACSI at its formation was to improve the health outcomes of Indigenous Peoples, either through improved encounters between Indigenous clients and health care providers or by health care providers becoming health advocates for Indigenous communities.

A logo for ACSI was created by the Indigenous artist Joseph Sagaj. The circle represents the Indigenous concept of holistic health in the form of a medicine wheel with four quadrants representing physical, cognitive, emotional, and spiritual health. The moccasin in the centre indicates that to improve Indigenous health, one needs to "walk in their shoes," and the message should be embraced by all races, white, oriental, black and brown, which are the stick figures holding hands. Finally, just above the shoelaces, there is a rising sun with its rays pointing forward, indicating enlightenment.

My role in the project was that of an ally and facilitator; the teachers would be Indigenous, and they would decide on the curriculum.

The first part of the curriculum focussed on the colonial and postcolonial policies and attitudes that determined the access to health services of the Indigenous communities. This was followed by health and wellness-based perspectives, conveying the Indigenous people's concepts of health and healing practices, including ceremonies, circles, healing lodges, etc. Through a process of self-reflection and acknowledging their own cultural values and the many diverse histories and cultures relating to First Nations, Inuit, and Métis people, the curriculum attempted to create a process through which learners could identify more closely with their Indigenous clients.

The success of the initiative was dependent on the ability of the volunteer instructors' knowledge and skills. We recruited thirty-two Indigenous instructors, graduates from post-secondary institutions in the geographic areas where the colleges and universities were located. Training and support were led by two Indigenous academicians who had developed the materials. We also developed and published several promotional videos that, along with our development of a dedicated website, established an easily accessible internet presence. Sessions were held in various colleges and universities throughout Ontario, with most sessions held in the southern Ontario region. Our preceptors delivered sessions to learners in several health science streams, including nursing, naturopathic medicine, chiropractic medicine, and medicine.

Our feedback reports indicated that the Indigenous Cultural Safety Initiative of AHT did change learner attitudes toward Indigenous clients, increased learner knowledge of Indigenous health and history and that the volunteer Indigenous instructors did effectively teach the subject matter.

The above pictorial diagram shows what students liked most about the program.

The ACSI was an ambitious program with an initial goal to reach at least forty percent of all health sciences programs across Ontario colleges and universities in less than eighteen months. In retrospect, while this goal was laudable, it was not achievable due to the initiative's short time frame. There were two plausible reasons that could be the cause of the initiative not being widely adopted. First, it is challenging to introduce change into the existing culture of postsecondary institutions. Apparently, demands on time with existing curriculum requirements did not leave adequate room for this initiative to be introduced. It was also suggested that for the institutions, cultural safety was not seen as an important aspect of teaching. The uptake numbers may also suggest that, in some institutions, there may have been a lack of information about the Initiative.

At the end of this pilot project in 2014, the Initiative was fortunate to have signed a partnership agreement with the Indigenous People's Education Circle, a group of committed Indigenous professionals in Ontario's colleges. They took over the program moving forward, and they would act as catalysts and provide the teaching in their respective colleges.

In December 2015 Canada's Truth and Reconciliation

Commission Report came out about the detailed history and condition of the Indigenous people. It is a harrowing document, and its Call to Action at the end states the following: "We call upon all levels of governments to provide cultural competency training for all health care professionals." (Action #23)

The Report has provided the impetus for developing accredited cultural safety programs across Canada. As one of the pioneers in this effort, today I feel satisfied that, finally, the educational institutions have heeded the call for the inclusion of the Indigenous Cultural Safety program in their curricula. My efforts, it seems, were not in vain.

7

Why Are They Dying Young? Urban Indigenous Health Strategy

Anishnawbe Health Toronto (AHT), where I began work as a primary care physician immediately after my retirement in 2001, is a community health centre serving mainly the inner-city urban Indigenous population. It was established in 1982 by a visionary elder, Joe Sylvester, initially as a research project on diabetes, when it became clear that the Indigenous community needed a more comprehensive approach to health care. AHT was incorporated in 1984. One of its objectives as stated was, "To recover, record, and promote traditional Indigenous practices where possible and appropriate."

In 1989, having successfully secured resources from the Ontario Ministry of Health, AHT became recognized and funded as a community health centre. Today, AHT promotes traditional Indigenous practices (such as smudging, drumming, the sunrise ceremony, the full moon ceremony). Its health care model is based on traditional practices and approaches and is reflected in the design of its programs and services (www.aht.ca). AHT continues to grow to meet the needs of the community it serves. A significant number of clients they serve have multiple chronic physical and mental health issues, are homeless, and live below the poverty line. Clients have varied Indigenous identities, such as First Nations individuals belonging to various nations with or without status, Métis, and Inuit. Many of them keep moving from one city to another, across the province and within the country, and a significant number of them commute to and from their home communities.

For a city the size of Toronto (2.3 million people), the Indigenous community is relatively small (40,000–60,000). Whenever there is an announcement of a death or a memorial service for a deceased Indigenous person, the centre receives a request for it to be posted on its general bulletin board. I was occasionally invited to memorial services by family members of my deceased patients to speak about them. This is rather unheard of in mainstream medical practice, but it was an honour bestowed upon me by the grieving families. One fall, in 2009, I received two such invitations in the span of a month to speak at the memorial services for my patients whom I had known well. It struck me that a few of our health centre patients were dying at a relatively young age, which raised a serious question—why were they dying young? What social factors were contributing to these early deaths?

To understand this phenomenon, I asked the clinic secretary whether she kept the death records of our patients. Fortunately, she did and promptly provided me with them. As a professor emeritus at the University of Toronto, I often got requests from students to spend their elective time with me during their residency-training program. I was fortunate to have such a request from Dr Rajbir Klair, who was in his final year of residency in family practice. He had only three weeks of elective at his disposal at the time, and after seeking permission from my executive director Joe Hester, I asked him whether he could review the records of those clinic patients who had died in the last two years. He was happy to do so and worked with me on the project until its conclusion.

I had developed significant understanding of most of the medical causes of death in Indigenous communities, so I shifted my focus to uncovering the root causes. Initially, we believed we might understand the deceased patients by exploring their social media and news media profiles. However, many of our patients were extremely marginalized, so we abandoned that enquiry route. Meanwhile, I had another member join my team, Allison Reeves, who had worked with me on the Indigenous Cultural Safety Initiative and was now finishing her doctoral thesis in clinical psychology.

Allison Reeves, Rajbir Klair, and I decided to quantify the health impact of the urban environments in which many Indigenous Peoples lived, specifically in Toronto. The study was focused on two things: to look at the age and sex of the deceased, and to discover the root cause for the high incidence of deaths within the Indigenous community, for which we needed to study the lives of the deceased individuals while they were alive. Along came Harvey Manning, an Indigenous social worker who had extensive experience dealing with the Indigenous homeless population and knew the Indigenous community in Toronto extremely well. He conducted an in-depth inquiry into the life experiences and social circumstances of twenty deceased people by connecting with close relatives and friends who knew the deceased intimately. While Indigenous people living on reserves may experience negative health outcomes due to lack of accessible health services, this should not be the case in an urban centre such as Toronto.

A total of 43 cases were considered—28 male and 15 female patients—and consisted of Status and Non-Status First Nations, Métis, and Inuit peoples. We contacted all other Indigenous social services to provide a list of individuals who had died in the past two years and had received services from their agency. We requested that they only provide the deceased individuals' sex and dates of birth and death. We received information on another 63 individuals from three Indigenous social service organizations in the Greater Toronto Area, thus making our sample a total of 109 individuals.

Analyzing the data, we found that the average age of death for the 109 individuals (62 males and 47 females) was 37 years. This number obviously represents a sample restricted to the Indigenous individuals who had used health and social services in the Greater Toronto Area. Nevertheless, the disparity between this age and the average age of death for a Torontonian (75 years) was vast. We found that the causes of death correlated directly with the conditions of homelessness, physical abuse, and substance use. Given Toronto's available health and social services, this trend was truly alarming.

A Human Perspective

We were already aware of the debilitating effects of the social environments of many Indigenous Peoples through their heart-wrenching stories told by family and friends. The stories, honest and shocking, spanned hundreds of different experiences, each generating a unique sense of revulsion. I would like to share some of the most poignant interview excerpts.

Many participants spoke of the individual, family, and community impacts of the government assimilation policies. One participant described the family impact of losing children to the residential school system:

> [The deceased] remembered as each of the older children were taken away from the mother—the parents—going to residential school until it came down to [the deceased] and [brother]. And he and [brother] got taken together at the same time, and they were the last two kids that the mother had in her care. So, it was hard on his mother, he

remembers, as she watched each of her children get taken away.

> I went to residential school and the things that happened there I can't . . .

> [The deceased's] brother was [raped] by the priest there. And her other sister just talks about it, but they don't . . . they lost the family bond. And, uh, so they don't really talk to each other, even to this day.

The subject of living in non-Indigenous communities also came up, the effects especially disastrous for the Indigenous children's school performance:

> Our parents didn't put a lot on us as far as going to school, and we actually missed so much school. And then school being so traumatic—going to a non-Native school and being the only Natives . . . we had suffered so much racism, discrimination, oppression, that we just began to really hate who we were . . . and that's just in the school setting!

The ways in which many of the subjects dealt with their stress also made it clear how so many of the subjects had problems with substance addiction.

> So [the deceased] was very sad. And you know what? That sadness—we understand how—it affects the spirit and the emotions like that. Her mind . . . she turned to try to escape it by partying and having a good time.

> I don't think [the deceased] could let himself go to that painful place inside himself that would have helped him in this life. Some people can't do that—they can never go there. It's like he trained himself at a young age somehow

to never go to that place. And he'd rather block it with the drugs and alcohol or just keep doing what he's doing.

Many participants also discussed domestic abuse, depicting extremely horrific childhood experiences:

> Oh my god! That man was the most violent man I could ever imagine! As little kids, he would beat [the deceased and I] up! [. . .] He was a horrible, horrible violent man. He was also a sexual predator. [. . .] My mom, I guess she tried to protect us, and he beat the crap out of her. [. . .] She said she was leaving, and she told us to stay 'cause she was so scared he was going to kill us all.

> But my dad would beat my mom bad in front of us. Like, we'd watch it.

Perhaps the most terrifying of the stories presented by the participants were those of the widespread and blatant sexual abuse many Indigenous had faced as children:

> . . . And [the deceased] was placed in a foster family with his sister. And the man—the foster dad—was raping his sister all along.

Finally, what truly brought attention to the fact that more had to be done to help the Indigenous community was that many of them did not pursue therapy because therapy was not welcoming enough. Feeling trapped in grief and unable to move forward on the healing journey was a common theme described by participants in this study. Experiences of trauma and addiction also undermined the self-esteem of many of the deceased:

> He was in a healing lodge when I met him, back in the 80s. And he did go to treatment. But he couldn't—he

would only last a few months or whatever. But would always walk out the door. He just couldn't seem to get down—there was something blocking him, truly letting himself really go deeper.

He just wouldn't even try to recover at that point. 'Cause he said it was too late. There was no point anymore. [. . .] And I think that you kind of reach a point where . . . to me, he was just tired. He was tired of trying. Tired of trying to be sober. Tired of trying to live a healthy life.

The study also suggests that the colonial messages that permeated Indigenous communities dictate these Indigenous people's desire to be less Indigenous and more white. Moreover, they are tasked with having to be wealthy and competing in the capitalist economy. The following quote summarizes the kind of identity loss that many of the deceased experienced in their lives because of not being connected to their culture:

That's inter-generational—you know, internalized oppression is always inter-generational. It's all from colonial crap that everyone wants to be white and rich. And we're never going to be white enough or rich enough.

Using root cause analysis theory, several recurring themes presented themselves as contributing to patient deaths, as depicted in the figure below. We called this the Delayed Tsunami Effect because of the insidious effects of colonial policies on Indigenous population even centuries later.

Root Cause Analysis of the Impact of Colonialism on Indigenous Health: Delayed Tsunami Effect

An overarching theme of the interviews was chronic stress. Many factors, namely domestic and sexual abuse as children, the exposure to substance abuse, the lack of family bonds and an inability to address their problems, led to the propagation of this stress throughout the deceased individuals' lives. The lack of resources and the social isolation these individuals experienced created large voids in their psyche. Most individuals could also recount numerous instances of racial and cultural discrimination, and the constant battles they were forced to engage in and their destructive nature.

A recurring echo in the interviews was the fact that if there had been access or connection to Indigenous healing processes for mental, emotional, and spiritual traumas, it could have staved off deaths. But the widespread cultural disruption that the governments exerted had succeeded in tearing its way through the cultural bonds of many Indigenous Peoples. The lack of internal healing due to the lack of access only served to accelerate this slide into oblivion.

Advocating for Health of Urban Indigenous Peoples

Over the last forty years, much attention has been paid to the health status of Indigenous communities living on the "reserve." Under the Canadian Constitution Act 1982, the federal government is responsible for the health of Indigenous people living on the reserve. Unfortunately, the Indigenous people living in urban settings were neglected by mainstream health and social services. Urban Indigenous leaders, understanding the need for culturally sensitive services, had developed different programs and services within the existing institutions and, where feasible, their own health and social services. Over the years, they established friendship centres for cultural revival and a safe place to practice their traditions, songs, and dances.

Having personally witnessed the pain and suffering that they went through, I felt a stark need for fair treatment when it came to the health of urban Indigenous people. As Rudy Ruettiger wrote, "When you achieve one dream, dream another. Getting what you want is only a problem if you have nowhere to go next. Dreaming is a lifetime occupation."

I dreamt obsessively about an equitable and harmonious environment for the Indigenous people of Canada. And for this, I advocated that the Public Health Branch, Ontario Ministry of Health, and the local Public Health Units focus on the health of Indigenous peoples in both urban and adjacent First Nations communities that did not have the necessary infrastructure. I was aware that local governments were always concerned that working with Indigenous communities would create a jurisdictional dispute among federal, provincial and local governments. However, this should not be insurmountable if goodwill existed at all three government levels. In the 1980s, I was upset when I learned that the City of Toronto Public Health Department had tied up with a city in a South

American country to help augment their public health infrastructure. Not that this city in South America should not get help from our rich resources, but I felt that the public health unit was neglecting its fundamental duty to look after the Indigenous Peoples right in its own city! Charity must begin at home.

When I worked as a special advisor to the deputy minister at the Indigenous Health Branch of Health Canada in 2007–08, I had several meetings with the Assembly of First Nations to see how public health needs could best be met by cooperation and devising a synergy of all three levels of governments with Indigenous communities. We never agreed and were unable to produce a solution. Unfortunately, local health units did not address the health issues of urban Indigenous people because they were unaware of their needs, jurisdictional issues always caused problems, and perhaps the Indigenous were not considered a priority population. Never one to quit despite odds, I continued to move forward with my causes.

The overwhelmingly scarring experiences that many of the subjects and their loved ones had faced created a chilling picture in our study. I strongly felt that the study's findings should generate public discourses leading to an action plan, if not everywhere, at least in Toronto. Armed with this study, I was sure to have a better chance at persuading the authorities concerned.

Fortunately, the City of Toronto had declared the period 12 November 2013 to 12 November 2014 as the Year of Truth and Reconciliation. It seemed apt to have the city effect change to reinforce this reconciliatory gesture. Along with my colleagues, I kick-started attempts at gaining exposure by presenting our research findings to the City of Toronto's Board of Health and the Indigenous Affairs Committee.

The Public Health Unit of the City of Toronto had just assembled a small team to develop a strategic plan to address the Indigenous people's issues in their area. They had no definite plan yet. As I was well acquainted with the Medical Officer of Health, David McEwan, another former student of mine, I got myself invited to present my study with one condition imposed by him—that I didn't make any recommendations. This was hard for me, but I reluctantly agreed to their request. A foot in the door was better than none. Along with my colleagues, I presented our findings in December 2013. I also got myself invited to the Toronto Central Local Health Integrating Network (LHIN), a planning body for allocating health care resources in the City of Toronto. The chair of their board and chief executive director, Camille Orridge (yet another former student of mine), were sympathetic to my cause.

My presentations led to the public health agency cooperating with the local health-planning agency to develop a strategic plan to improve Indigenous health. As with all agencies, their wheels rotated slowly. Every chance I got, I reminded them to move forward and not get into the "paralysis by analyses" mode. They tolerated my not-so-gentle reminders.

Though I was confident that my project would receive media attention and even action, I was wrong to assume so. I then decided to employ a more assertive tactic. I wrote to the chair of the Urban Indigenous Affairs Committee of the City of Toronto to provide me with an opportunity to present the study to them. In planning our presentation and recommended amendments to the current city policy, we kept the significance of the Year of Truth and Reconciliation in mind. Councillor Michael Layton, head of the Indigenous Affairs Committee for Toronto, had in fact been the spokesperson for the City at the announcement of the special Year. This is what he had proclaimed:

> This year-long proclamation acknowledges those injustices of the residential school system on Indigenous

Peoples. It also adds to the ongoing work the City is doing to build strong working relationships with Indigenous communities and partnerships for the development of successful programs and policies.

> . . . the City reaffirms its commitment to implement-
> ing the framework through activities such as education
> of the Toronto Public Service on Indigenous history;
> Indigenous employment strategy; representation of
> Indigenous Peoples at City agencies and corporations;
> and partnership and capacity building.[4]

Using his words as a guide, we created a set of concrete recommendations that would help the City achieve its goals. The city's pledge certainly gave more weight to the gravity of our findings and recommendations. The committee was taken aback by them and agreed to forward them to the Toronto Mayor's Executive Council. They also instructed various departments to act upon our recommendations, including Toronto Public Service, the Department of Homeless Persons, the Department of Low-income Housing, the Department of Parks & Recreation, Toronto Public Health, Toronto Central Local Health Integrating Network, and the Toronto District School Board. In addition to forwarding our report, the committee posted a copy of our report on their website, which turned out to be an incredible boost to the topic's exposure. Still, we did not see any concrete action from the city's public health department. Several months of gruelling, sincere work didn't seem to be paying off. I was quite disappointed again.

However, my disappointment was soon replaced with hope. In June 2014, three months after our presentation, things perked up. It just so happened that Jordan Chittley, a news reporter with the

---

4   https://nationtalk.ca/story/toronto-proclaims-year-of-truth-and-reconciliation-
    acknowledging-impact-of-canadas-residential-schools

Canadian Television Network (CTV), stumbled across our study and was amazed by our finding that the average age of death for our subjects was 37 years. However, he erroneously confused the average age of death with life expectancy. But to our advantage the story was highly publicized and picked up by several news outlets before Mr Chittley's headline could be corrected. But it did bring much-desired attention to the debilitating social stigma concerning the Indigenous in Toronto and created an unexpected momentum in our movement.

The report led to several interviews for my colleagues and me, allowing us to draw even more exposure to the subject and present our recommendations for helping the injured heal through a widely digested medium. Newspapers like Toronto-based *Metro News* reported that "health outcomes among Indigenous Peoples are poor and there are many premature deaths of Indigenous Peoples in Toronto," creating a large amount of public support for our goals. The issue garnered national attention as well, with CBC featuring it during their prime-time evening news; their website said that "many of the Indigenous Peoples who had died prematurely in Toronto had attended a residential school," which provided extra fodder for the national debate. Wab Kinew, an Indigenous reporter and now a leader of the New Democratic Party in Manitoba, also interviewed me in 2019. The widespread publicity brought support and further credibility to our study and the recommendations we made.

So far, the City of Toronto has implemented several of our recommendations. The report from the Medical Officer of the Board of Health, City of Toronto, dated 6 November 2015, stated the following:

> On December 9th, 2013, Anishnawbe Health Toronto (AHT) presented their research to the Board of Health on premature deaths among Toronto's Indigenous

community. This presentation reinforced the need for Toronto Public Health to continue partnering with AHT and the Toronto Central Local Health Integration Network (TC LHIN) in the establishment of a comprehensive, community-led and integrated Indigenous Health Strategy to improve health outcomes for Toronto's Indigenous community.

Following this, the Toronto Indigenous Health Advisory Circle (TIHAC) was established to recognize that the Indigenous Health Strategy (IHS) must be led by community members themselves. On 23 January 2015, TIHAC was officially launched at the Native Canadian Centre of Toronto. The day included a sacred fire, sunrise ceremony, pipe ceremony, and a community feast. After much deliberation, in 2016, Toronto's first Indigenous Health Strategy (2016–2021) was released. It is an insightful document and, besides addressing the health issues, it has paid a great deal of attention to social determinants of health such as education, employment, racism, and discrimination.

8

Highs and Lows

It is not the critic who counts, not the man who points out how the strong man stumbles, or where the doer of deeds could have done them better. The credit belongs to the man in the arena, whose face is marred by dust and sweat and blood, who strives valiantly, who errs and comes short again and again, who knows the great enthusiasms, the great devotions, who spends himself in a worthy cause. Who at the best knows in the end the triumph of high achievement, and who at the worst, if he fails, at least fails while daring greatly, so that his place shall never be with those cold and timid souls who have never known neither victory nor defeat.

THEODORE ROOSEVELT

What is success without failure? Though I am fortunate to have been able to realize many of my dreams—some that I never thought would come true, there have been incidents where despite my efforts, I couldn't achieve what I had set out to do. The exhilaration of a win is always preceded by the disenchantment of a defeat. What is important is that I always learnt from them.

When I was working as a visiting pediatric consultant at the Sioux Lookout Zone in Northwest Ontario, many of the remote

Indigenous communities were accessible only by small planes. There were no landing strips. During this period, gasoline sniffing in children as young as four was almost epidemic in scale in a few communities. Gasoline contained lead, and that meant chronic lead poisoning, resulting in impairment of cognitive functions. Whenever I visited such a community, children were brought to me with learning and behaviour problems. While I tried to mitigate the individual issue, it dawned on me that this was a public health issue, which needed public health solutions to prevent it.

During my pediatric training in Chicago, I had treated chronic lead poisoning in children who had ingested wall paint. I was unfamiliar with gasoline sniffing in children, its consequences, and preventive programs. However, one day I chanced upon a study that showed that Australia too had a similar problem in their teenage Aborigines living near an airport who sniffed airline fuel to get "high." To deter its use, the Australian authorities used an additive in the jet fuel to provoke nausea and vomiting in those who sniffed it. This seemed a great idea, and I thought we should consider the same. But how does one know which gasoline is transported to those communities? On further enquiry, I discovered that in Canada gasoline for agricultural use and that which is supplied to First Nations communities was separated for tax purposes by colour coding.

I asked the Petroleum Association of Canada, based in Calgary, for their help in putting additives into gasoline destined for the First Nations communities. I had a few meetings with their chief executive officer; while they were willing and eager to help me, they needed more research and the necessary funding. When I approached the local Indigenous community with my ideas, they expressed reservations. Their concern was about how the additive would impact their machinery, such as snowmobiles and motorboats, which were vital for survival. They also needed more assurance that the additive would be safe for their children. But I lacked the know-how and resources.

Ten years down the road in 1993, I was moved while watching a television program about an epidemic of gasoline sniffing in Innu children and young adults living in Davis Inlet in Labrador. The situation was so bad that the community evacuated the affected children and young adults for treatment to addiction centres and hospitals far away from their communities.

Why had I failed?

Let me first describe the community. It was very remote, with very little infrastructure other than a school and a small health clinic staffed by nurses, with monthly visits by an itinerant physician like me. Nurses, doctors, and teachers working in these communities generally mean well, but they, like other Canadians, lack the necessary knowledge.

At that time, I did not appreciate the need for community engagement and community development before imposing my solution, i.e., putting an additive into their gasoline.

I recall an incident from the early 1990s in Darwin, Australia, when I had visited as a World Health Organization Fellow. My host took me to a hospital built specifically for their Indigenous people. It was a beautiful structure; however, I hardly saw patients in their rooms. I saw them sitting or lying on hospital grounds under the shades of trees. They were accustomed to living in open spaces; unless very sick, they preferred the outdoors. But the Australian authorities in Canberra who designed the hospital were unaware of this.

I am not trying to find an excuse for my behaviour. The Indigenous people were rightly apprehensive about an unknown additive ruining their snowmobiles and small boats, which were their only means of hunting and fishing. They were probably afraid that their children would get bored as there were no other means to keep them busy and they would resort to other dangerous activities. What they needed were infrastructure and organized activities for children. Obviously, I ought to have involved the community to earn their trust. One of the Innu elders commented on the possible solution for the incident in 2017: "We are Innu. We cannot be healthy or successful in life without understanding and embracing our culture, our language and our connection with our land and animals."

Goodwill and good intentions are not sufficient for success. The following is an account of how the dominant society's sociopolitical construct influenced an outcome.

During my visits to the Sioux Lookout Zone, I grasped the fact that to improve Indigenous health, a multi-pronged approach was necessary, including addressing the social determinants of health. I would invariably visit the local cooperative store to learn the cost and types of foods available. Most of them were imported from the south by air. This knowledge provided me with glimpses of the Indigenous people's nutritional habits and an insight into the cost of living. Food prices were exorbitant, on an average three to four times more compared to those in the south. Many were suffering from iron deficiency.

A kernel of an idea was planted in my mind. If one could build a bakery in these remote First Nations communities, fortifying the bread with iron would not just help take care of nutritional needs but also create sorely needed employment, and instil pride in self-sufficiency and even in eating fresh bread!

In the summer of 1986, unexpectedly I received a phone call from someone from Media.com, a US-based company in Canada mainly in the business of advertisement via billboards on prominent

TO CHANGE THE WORLD

sites, including bus stops. On behalf of the Gannett Foundation, he told me, they were soliciting initiatives to help marginalized communities. Someone familiar with my work had suggested approaching me. He informed me that there would be a competition among the submissions from Toronto. He requested that I submit a letter of intent if I were interested. The proposed funding for the project was about $100,000.

Right away, I thought of submitting my idea for a bakery in a remote First Nations community. While I was not sure about the exact location, I knew I had good relations with the Chiefs and Band Councils in a few communities, namely Bearskin Lake, Kitchenuhmaykoosib Aaki (Big Trout Lake). I knew that they would at least consider my request. Before submitting a letter of intent, I consulted my department chair, Dr Mary Jane Ashley, for her approval. The business venture of developing a bakery would be beyond my scope of work. I convinced her that this project was about tackling the social determinants of health. It would provide employment and empower the First Nations community; it was a true health and social development project relevant to the department's mandate. She trusted my instinct and gave me the green light. The Foundation received some fifty letters of intent from Toronto, from which my project won the competition. Similar competitions were held in Winnipeg and Montreal and a winner was chosen for each city. Following this, only one winner was to be chosen from Canada and my project was chosen. As a result, I was asked to make a full-scale application.

Let me reveal a secret: I am a chapati eater. I do not like ordinary bread and hardly ever eat it, and here I was planning a bakery business! To develop the full application, I needed to provide a rationale for the project, receive support letters from non-Indigenous community leaders, develop partnerships, and receive endorsements from the participating First Nations community and their regional political organization Nishnawbe Aski Nations, which represents 51 First Nation communities across Treaty 9 and Treaty 5 areas of Northern Ontario.

Bread is a staple diet amongst northern Indigenous people. On an average, each one eats two loaves of bread per week, amounting to 100 loaves per year per person. Thus, in the Sioux Lookout Zone alone, 12,000 (combined population of sixteen reserves in 1986) consumed 1.2 million loaves of bread a year. The cost of bread ranged from $1.75 to $2.35 per loaf, averaging $2.00 per loaf. Thus, these communities spent annually almost $2.4 million on bread alone. All the bread was flown in from either Thunder Bay (400 km from Sioux Lookout) or Winnipeg (450 km). The grocery stores diverted the profits from bread back to the parent companies in the south. Besides bread, these communities consumed hot dogs and hamburgers, bannocks (an indigenous bread) and cookies; children and young adults constituted fifty percent of the population. This would make it easy for the successful bakery to diversify into other baking goods.

The production of bread was relatively easy. It did not need high technology or technical workforce. Being part of the staple diet, the need for bread would be continuous. Being self-sufficient in one important area, such as producing one's own bread, would provide people with a sense of accomplishment and empowerment and stimulate other reserves to emulate. Success with the bakery would also stimulate them to start other small-scale industries such as raising chickens. I believed that developing employment opportunities on reserves will enhance the survival of the First Nations' cultures by enabling more people to live and work in their communities. It will also decrease migration from the reserve to urban centres, and those who migrate will be better prepared for employment there.

To help gain momentum, I solicited support letters from Indigenous and non-Indigenous persons and organizations to indicate the project's worthiness and was overwhelmed by their enthusiastic support. In her letter, Chief Rosie S Mosquito from the Bearskin Lake Band said, "The reservations throughout Northern Ontario are generally disadvantaged in developing viable and successful economic development projects. The lack of funding to cover start-up costs is one of the primary reasons. This has certainly been the experience of the Bearskin Lake Band when we tried to develop a bakery several years ago."

Getting endorsements is always an advantage but not knowing how things work is the biggest disadvantage. I was ignorant about developing and running a business, and so I needed help in making a business plan and the bakery infrastructure. I did not know what it entailed—the equipment required, the necessary ingredients for making bread, staffing, staff training, budgeting, and marketing. I also had my teaching and administrative responsibilities as director of the largest residency program in North America, training public health physicians, and teaching undergraduate and graduate courses. I had scant support staff. Fortunately, when I was venting with my colleagues at the lunch table, Dr Mabel Halliday told me that her husband, a baker, had just retired, and she would ask him whether he would volunteer his services. The next day she announced he would join my team.

Mr W Halliday came with impeccable credentials. He was a bakery specialist who had retired as manager of Instore Bakeries (Food City) for the Ontario division of Oshawa Group Ltd; he had been director of the Retail Division of the Bakery Council of Canada and editor of *Little Dough Maker*, a publication of Bakery Production of Ontario. He provided invaluable help in developing the proposal.

I was still left with not knowing how to make a business plan. Someone suggested I contact an organization of retired chief executive officers known as the Canadian Executive Service Organization (CESO). This organization generally provided volunteer help for projects in developing countries and far north in the Inuit communities. I decided to approach them. They heeded my request and assigned two volunteers, Mrs M Tucker (a retired English teacher who had worked overseas), and Mr D G Scott (FCA, a volunteer consultant with a financial and administrative background and retired president and CEO of a major Canadian printing company with over 2000 employees).

Mr Scott worked relentlessly with me. I was under the impression that if we were to make bread at the local level, the price of a loaf of bread would go down. To my surprise, that was not so. Every ingredient needed had to be brought by air from elsewhere. The other surprise was that there was no electric grid in those communities; a special line for the proposed bakery site would be required. The next challenge was communicating with the communities. This was difficult, as I was 1500 km away from the proposed Indigenous communities. It cost approximately $3500 for a round trip from Toronto, in case I needed personal meetings. When I reached there I had to beg the nursing station for accommodation in lieu of clinical service.

If that were not enough, I also had to develop a coalition to make sure if funded, I had a group who would guide and support the project. There were several organizations such as Indigenous, voluntary and government that were involved in the project.

From the beginning, I held the view that this project should be owned and operated by Indigenous people, and I was there merely to help. I needed an Indigenous advisory committee to make major decisions. I recruited such a team.

With all these plans and the information under my belt, I finally submitted a completed application to the foundation. As the Gannett Foundation is US-based and unknown to me, I competed with applicants from the fifty American states for the final five successful applications they intended to fund. Their representative told me that the bakery project was rated in the top five by their review committee and it was sent to their board for final approval. However, the board decided against the project as it was in a remote corner of Canada—its benefactor Media.com would not receive the desired publicity. This was a great disappointment for the Indigenous communities and me!

Following this, I tried several venues, including the Government of Ontario's Small Business Development Program for Northern Ontario, which was geared toward establishing small businesses with private ownership in the north. The fund had an unspent $2.5 million. But they only funded businesses with private ownership. I was asked if I could convince the bands to float shares and establish the bakery as a private business corporation. However, the concept of individual ownership was at variance with Indigenous values and culture, where the ownership is communal, including their houses! The project was finally aborted.

Compared to the gasoline sniffing project, I had followed all the required practices, such as community engagement, community mobilization and cooperation, a proper business plan, and receiving wide support from both Indigenous and non-Indigenous opinion-makers. Where did I go wrong? I thought it a system failure. First, even though my project received accolades from the reviewers of the Gannett Foundation, and was placed among the five finalists, the decision to reject it was based on other considerations. The Ontario Business Development Corporation's conditions of private corporate ownership went against Indigenous values. The only solace I had was that I now own a baker's hat given to me by my residents upon my stepping down as the program director with a broken dream! But I still have not given up the bakery idea.

It is always gratifying to be awarded recognition; though one should be wary that it does not get into your head, create a sense of hubris, a feeling that you can solve anything, that it was only you all the way without goodwill or assistance from others. As I have said, bringing about change is a slow process; it is especially difficult if you come from a different culture and history, are of the "wrong" colour, speak differently. But recognition in any case is a transitory phenomenon. What remains are memories and the satisfaction of having done something.

One day in 1987, I was invited by the National Aboriginal Council on Disability to present my findings on Indigenous disability at Kahnawake First Nations community near Montreal. The Métis physician who was their consultant was also in attendance. At the end of the meeting, I was taken to a private setting by their elder and asked whether I would consider being their consultant. I asked why, for they already had one of their own. He hesitantly told me that I thought more like them, while their own did not. Such moments made me feel I was on the right path; I may not be one of them, but I was accepted as a friend. I was given a spirit name by an Indigenous healer: Maamaazhii N'iamh Manidoo Aki, which means "Conquered his Spirit on Earth," because when you conquer your spirit, you truly know who you are. It also means: "One comes from the core of the earth to bring this name. You sit with the Bear Clan. They are big bears. Bears are associated with healing power."

On 23 September 2004, Sudha and I came home late after spending the evening with friends. There was a message on our phone, it told me to call Prime Minister Paul Martin's office upon my return, irrespective of the time. I was intrigued, to say the least. It was around 11 p.m. when I called the Prime Minister's Office; no one answered, so I left a message and received a call back within fifteen minutes. An important-sounding person swore me to secrecy and told me about the impending announcement of the creation of the Public Health Agency of Canada (PHAC) the next day. He had a few concerns, and I was asked my opinion. I told him I had a few suggestions. 1) As the proposed agency was being created in the aftermath of the disastrous SARS epidemic and Naylor's Report on the Renewal of Public Health in Canada, I wanted to make sure that the focus was not only on the surveillance and prevention of infectious diseases but also on chronic diseases. I gave examples of how infectious diseases like AIDS, and hepatitis B and C, which started as acute conditions, have now joined the list of chronic diseases. (This was experienced again with long-term COVID 19.) I was asked if I would fax them a list of acute diseases becoming chronic. 2) My second suggestion was that in my experience, Indigenous health issues in our country were completely ignored in the mandates of many Canadian programs and were mere afterthoughts. I strongly urged them not only to include them but also to make sure that progress on them be reported annually. I was happy to see in days to come that both my points were incorporated. The first Chief Medical Officer of Canada's Public Health Agency was Dr David Butler-Jones, a former student of mine.

One day in 2007, I received a call at my clinic office at AHT from the Assistant Deputy Minister, Ian Porter, asking me if I would consider the position of Chief Medical Officer of Community Health in First Nations and Inuit Health Branch of Health Canada; now known as Indigenous Services Canada. I was flattered, but I had then reached the age of seventy. Reason prevailed and I told him that I was not looking for a job at my age and had no intention of moving to Ottawa. We had a lovely discussion, and he concluded our conversation by saying that I should still consider his offer and he would call again. I considered his offer further, consulted with trusted friends, and understood that this was a chance to influence Canada's health policies. In our subsequent discussions it became evident that they had advertised the job and interviewed three or four candidates. None of them met with the search committee's criteria, and somehow my name had been suggested as a desirable candidate. To be a civil servant did not suit me, as I had a habit of speaking out. However, my convictions thrust upon me an alternative solution, that I work as a special advisor to him two days a week in Ottawa, and for the remaining three days, I continue to work at Anishnawbe Health Toronto as primary care physician. It was agreed.

For eighteen months I commuted to Ottawa every Sunday evening, returning to Toronto on Tuesday evening. Again, my wife thought, there go the so-called retirement or golden years when we could spend more time together. At times my sons told me to slow down, but they realized that work was more fulfilling for me than spending time on the golf course. The job in Ottawa was quite a learning experience for me, and I developed further respect for our civil service. It would be remiss of me if I did not mention one of my observations: three floors were occupied by civil servants in the branch where I worked, but there were only two "Indians" there: one was I, originally from India, and the other was a First Nations woman! So was the talk about employment equity, transfer of power, and inclusion mere platitude?

After my second retirement, in August 2017, I was at the birthday party of a friend who was celebrating her eightieth birthday. As I entered the hall, I was greeted by Kanta Arora, a well-known South Asian anchor for Asia Television Network and the president of the

Toronto Netralya Lions Club, and Sudha Rastogi also a member of the club. In a secluded corner, they told me that the Netralya Lion's Club was interested in helping Indigenous peoples by raising funds for a worthwhile project. They were aware of my work with the Indigenous communities and were seeking guidance and help from me. *Netralya,* a Hindi word, means "house of eye or vision" and their focus was to improve vision care. I had several meetings with their board members, educating them about historical injustices Indigenous Peoples had suffered and explaining the necessity of building trust and relationship with the community. I introduced them to the executive directors and board members of AHT and Anishnawbe Health Foundation (AHF). As AHF was raising a ten-million-dollar fund for a new building for AHT, after several discussions their board decided to host a gala banquet to raise funds for two rooms to be devoted to vision care in the proposed new facility. The whole process took about eighteen months, and they raised $127,000 in 2018. It was a great experience for South Asian and Indigenous communities to build a trust relationship and since then the club has raised funds for various causes benefiting Indigenous communities.

Another event worth retelling is my encounter with one of the wealthiest families in Canada. While driving on Gerrard Street East in 2018, I saw a building named Sally Horsfall Eaton School of Nursing. The Eaton family for many years owned the landmark department store in downtown Toronto, and gave the name to the present Eaton Centre. I remember meeting Mrs Eaton some forty years ago and working with her for a conference on hearing-impaired children. We met again in 2007 very briefly at a dinner in honour of my late student, Dr Sheela Basrur. John Eaton, her husband, hosted the dinner as Chancellor of Toronto Metropolitan University. Knowing the Eaton family's philanthropic reputation,

I decided to contact her for our ten-million-dollar building campaign, and I invited her to visit our present health centre and assist in our campaign. While she graciously accepted the invitation, she said they had committed their foundation funds to other causes. I assured her all I wanted from her were goodwill and blessings. The executive director of our foundation, Julie Cookson, and I had a lovely luncheon meeting orienting her about the project but not soliciting any funds. Within two weeks of our luncheon, I got a phone call from her stating that she would commit $300,000 towards our campaign, provided we found matching donations over the next three years. We were able to match her funds in less than eighteen months.

9

The Disabled

As mentioned before, I had done a study on disabilities among First Nations people in the 1980s and subsequently became an honorary consultant on the Aboriginal National Disability Network. As a consultant I was invited by then President Joanne Francis of the Aboriginal National Disability Network to her home community, the Akwesasne First Nations community. At that time the Parliamentary Committee on Disability was conducting its public hearing on the subject in their community. Chief Mitchell knew of my presence in his community and asked me to prepare a brief on the subject. I said that the prevalence of disability in First Nations People is two to three times that of the national average, the age of onset of disability is earlier, and essentially there was a complete lack of preventive, curative and rehabilitations services, particularly in remote communities. I was immensely impressed with Chief Mitchell's grasp of the subject matter from my brief summary and by his oratory!

I have already described my futile attempt to prevent lead-poisoning in kids sniffing fuel. Then I learned that there was much to be done, but it had to be done with an understanding of the community involved.

Anishnawbe Health Centre, where I worked after my retirement from the university, had multidisciplinary assessment program for children having Fetal Alcohol Spectrum Syndrome (FASD) and as a pediatrician, I was the head of the program. Indigenous children with suspected FASD were referred to our clinic from the southwest and north for assessment and treatment plan. FASD occurs when a mother drinks alcohol during pregnancy, thus affecting the brain and physical features of the developing fetus. Upon birth, these affected children may exhibit several physical features and impaired cognitive functions depending upon the amount of alcohol consumed and the stage of pregnancy when consumption occurred. The impairment in cognitive functions and abnormal behaviour may not be evident until the child reaches school-going age. Upon referral by parents, physicians, schools or social agencies, our team assessed children suspected of exhibiting symptoms of FASD. Our team consisted of a traditional healer, a neuropsychologist, a social worker, an occupational therapist, the FASD program coordinator, a nurse, and me. The diagnosis depended on the mother's prenatal history of alcohol exposure. As many of these children were in the care of child welfare agencies or relatives, it was difficult to ascertain the mother's history of alcohol consumption during her pregnancy. At the end of the assessment, we held a case conference summarizing our diagnostic findings, confirming or denying that a child had FASD and providing a set of practical recommendations for managing the child in their community. A meeting with parents followed.

The following unsolicited response from one of the community teachers reflects their feelings towards our work.

Feb 26, 2013

Dear Dr Shah,

Today I attended a meeting you chaired, along with a team of others regarding J. I am a former teacher, now a friend of his mother T. As a teacher with the Toronto District School Board, I have attended many such meetings, but none conducted with as much care and compassion as you and your team exhibited today. These can be very formal affairs, as we know, and can feel quite uncomfortable for the parents and caregivers, but I feel you have a gift for putting them at ease. You phrased things in such a way that made it evident that you have taken the time to think about what it must be like to be receiving such difficult news for the first time. I am most thankful, though, for what you said to J's mother T at the very end. To tell her that it is not her fault that J most likely has FASD, and to tell her that you know that she would not intentionally harm her child, was one of the most important and compassionate things she probably ever heard from anyone in her life. I am so glad I was at the meeting because I hope to help reinforce that message and help her with the healing, she says she wants to do for herself. Thank you so much.

Sincerely, SM

Many of these children lacked what we call "executive functioning," which means they were unable to judge the consequence of their actions and hence became vulnerable to manipulations by others or by their desire for instant gratification. In doing so, they would commit a crime, be caught, get a criminal record, and even end up at a juvenile detention centre. This became particularly evident when they entered their teens. We were referred for assessment a sizeable number of teens who were not previously diagnosed. I was convinced that if the law enforcement officers knew about their condition, they would be more sympathetic in their approach. The judge would recommend their rehabilitation rather than sending them to detention centres. Therefore, I recommended that all our clients diagnosed with FASD wear a med-alert bracelet, so that the police would be alerted to their situation if they were caught. I met with resistance, the objection being that the bracelets would stigmatize the children. I still do not know what the right thing to do is.

We later started receiving referrals to assess adults who may have undiagnosed FASD; these referrals came from our own mental health departments and Indigenous agencies including the Aboriginal Legal Services Toronto (ALST). While Indigenous Peoples in Canada constitute about four percent of the total population, they represent about thirty percent of federal penitentiary inmates. We also realized that there were many Indigenous young adults in the prison system who may have FASD. They needed rehabilitation and not incarceration. I joined hands with Jonathan Rudin, a staff member at ALST, an eminent lawyer devoted to Indigenous Peoples, and we decided to address this issue by providing the necessary evidence. We decided to assess inmates who were on remand and may have undiagnosed FASD. And so, at the age of seventy-eight I visited all the jails in Greater Toronto Area, including one in Milton and Hamilton, for the assessment. It was quite an experience, beginning with the elaborate security check. A correctional officer led us to the medical facility or a designated room and provided me with the necessary equipment. The inmate was then brought in for examination.

The designated room allocated for the medical examination was a cage with a table and bench fixed firmly to the ground. The inmates, both men and women, we met were in their twenties and early thirties, very polite and with tragic, heart-wrenching stories. Their stories were collaborated from different sources. When our team provided their findings to the individual inmates at the end of the assessment, they were extremely grateful, and we even received many hugs. But somehow our project was plagued by unforeseen events and staff changes. When I retired at the age of eighty, the project had hardly moved forward. This unfinished initiative still haunts me.

As a family physician at Anishnawbe Health Toronto, I was required to fill out application forms for the Ontario Disability Support Program (ODSP) on behalf of Indigenous patients who were unable to work due to their disability. Individuals receiving ODSP were entitled to receive more government support than those who received welfare payment. This added payment helped individuals to cover necessary extra costs. Over the years I noticed that a fair number of these applications were rejected, particularly those related to mental health disabilities. I knew that those who assessed these applications at the Ontario Ministry of the Community and Social Services in Social Assistant Division had very little knowledge about the Indigenous situation. I offered my services to the director of the program Dr Andres Laxamana, who happened to be one of my former students, to educate these bureaucrats and held several sessions with them.

10

More Reflections

Faith Communities: Churches in the North

Resources for health, education, and social services are scarce in the northern communities; so are employment opportunities. As mentioned earlier, I had stopped visiting Sioux Lookout in 1990. I thought before I retired as a physician, I should visit there once more to witness the progress made over the past twenty-five years. It was most heartening to see the transformation of the old Sioux Lookout Zone Hospital; there was a new building, now called Sioux Lookout Meno Ya Win Health Centre; Meno Ya Win means health, wellness, well-being. The building was designed by world renowned Indigenous architect Douglas Cardinal and built in 2010 on the sacred and traditional territory of the Lac Seul Ojibwe Nation with four wings welcoming people from all directions. Besides Western health care, it also provided traditional foods, healing, and medicine. Indigenous voices had a major say in running the health centre.

During my visit, in 2015, I was assigned to visit a very remote and isolated First Nations community with a population of merely 250. One of the patients I saw in the nursing station was bed-ridden for a while and needed home visits to keep him socially connected. There were three churches in that small community and my client belonged to the Mennonite Church. I requested an appointment with his pastor; the pastor and his wife, both in their late twenties, were kind enough to offer to come to the nursing station. I narrated the concerns I had for my client, asking for their help, following which we had a lengthy conversation. At the end of the visit, while the pastor was getting up from his chair, he said, "Dr Shah, I am worried about you." I asked him why. He said he realized that I was not young, and I was a good man, but when I depart from the earth, I would not go to heaven because I did not belong to the Christian faith, and "only those who believe in Christ go to heaven." I replied, "My dear Pastor, please do not worry about me." And then I asked him if he knew that there were seven heavens, one for Christians, one for Muslims, one for Hindus, and so on, and assured him that if he believed that I was a good man, then surely one of these heavens would accept me. He was speechless!

I have visited quite a few remote and isolated communities during my career. I have met non-Indigenous peoples working there as teachers, nurses, nurse practitioners, clergies from various Christian faiths, Hudson Bay managers, pastors and priests and others. I was able to classify them into six categories, which I call my six M's: 1) Missionaries: individuals who in the truest sense were spiritual and interested in serving humanity; 2) Mercenaries: individuals whose primary interest lay in making good money in the north where they received higher salaries, almost free accommodation, and northern allowances so they could easily save money and go back south; 3) Megalomaniacs: those who thought they had all the solutions for Indigenous peoples' suffering, and that they were the saviours; 4) Misfits: these individuals were either running away from their problems such as alcoholism or hiding from the law; 5) Misinformed:

mainly young Canadians who had romantic notions of Indigenous communities in the north, and while they had good intentions, they were also ill-prepared for the isolation, harsh environment, and lack of resources; many of them were soon disillusioned and headed back home in a short time; 6) Mesmerized: individuals who truly loved living in the north and the lifestyle it afforded and settled down there.

Through my experience of working with Indigenous people, I have observed that even in the smallest communities in the north, there is more than one Christian church. Blessed are those who work there! Their main diocese supports these churches for their missionary work, and in the context of those communities, they remain relatively resource-rich. Over the years, I saw that the churches were more interested in expanding their congregation by converting Indigenous people rather than being involved in the public good. If they truly cared for humankind, they would put their resources together and help the inhabitants in many ways. Let me cite an example. During the visit described above, I regularly came across patients with substance-use disorders (addiction mainly related to prescribed pain medications) treated with an oral medication called Suboxone. Suboxone is used like methadone for opioid addiction, as a substitute that is slowly tapered off; it can be used in a smaller community and does not need a designated centre as is the case with individuals on methadone. I was asked to see them as they were scheduled to taper their drug dose, leading to its withdrawal. They had multiple nonspecific complaints, which were inexplicable. However, on reflection, it dawned on me that there were quite a few social and health issues that put people on opioid use to ease their pain or unhappiness. While opioids gave relief, they were also addictive, and here they were being treated for their addiction by Suboxone, which must be tapered off and eventually stopped. In the first place, as their life situation had not changed, they were afraid and did not know how they would cope when they stopped their medication. They needed survival skills and a meaningful engagement in their day-to-day life. I thought this local problem needed a local solution. As mentioned above, churches had more resources than the community.

If these churches came together with the Indigenous leaders and service providers, all would benefit. However, upon my return to Toronto, I found that while individuals in the hierarchy of churches liked the idea, there was no commitment. Ultimately, I decided to channel my energies elsewhere.

My work with different faith churches such as the United Church, the Anglican Church, and the Presbyterian Church has been rewarding; they have been extremely generous. My most memorable experience in working with the churches involved the late Anglican Archbishop Edward Scott. The Scott-McKay-Bain Health Panel was convened by the Indigenous Medical Services Branch of the Government of Canada and the Nishnawbe Aski Nation of northern Ontario in response to a hunger strike by the Aboriginal leaders in the Sioux Lookout Zone Hospital which is now known as Sioux Lookout Meno Ya Win Health Centre. In January 1988, five men from Sandy Lake First Nation—Josias Fiddler, Peter Goodman, Allen Meekis, Peter Fiddler and Luke Mamakeesic—went on a hunger strike to draw attention to years of worsening health care and deteriorating relations between First Nation communities and the Medical Services Branch of Health and Welfare Canada. Archbishop Scott was the lead commissioner; the other two members were the late Harry Bain from the Hospital for Sick Children, and Wally McKay, executive director of Tikinagan Child and Family Service. I was one of the research consultants on this project. One Saturday morning in the spring of 1989 I received a call from the archbishop asking me whether I could review the draft of their final report before it went to the printer next Monday. I asked him why. He replied, "While I trust my two other commissioners, I need an opinion from a neutral person like you." I was honored by his faith in me and said yes. He told me that the report would be delivered to my home in a short while. Two hours later my doorbell rang, and when I opened my door, to my astonishment I saw it was the archbishop himself with the report. This is one of the greatest examples of humility I have encountered. The report described the sorry state of the health services provided to the Indigenous peoples living in the isolated twenty-six communities and proposed solutions in the form of concrete suggestions, which included the establishment of the First Nations Health Authority led by Indigenous people.

In one of our discussions the archbishop spoke of how we all have unconscious bias. He was appointed by Prime Minister Mulroney as an envoy during the South African crisis before its independence. He said that during one of his trips to South Africa, while waiting at Nairobi airport for his onward flight, he picked up a newspaper. One headline was about the killing of two white nuns, another was about the killing of about one hundred Africans in Kenyan riots. On reading the headlines he initially felt tormented about the nuns' deaths. Then he thought of those Africans who had been killed. Right away, he realized that all those killed were the children of God and he should mourn equally for all life lost.

Fasting for Vision Quest

As mentioned earlier, I worked at the Anishnawbe Health Centre from 2001–2016. In May 2007, I was invited to fast by our traditional healer, Harry Snowboy, in Chisasibi, Quebec, as this was his community. Jane Harrison, the clinic manager, the healer's assistant, and our executive director, Joe Hester, were also invited to fast.

Many Indigenous communities practice the ritual of fasting every spring and fall. It consists of individuals going into the wilderness, staying in a small tent by themselves and fasting for three to seven days. During this period they meditate and seek visions from the Creator. At the end, all individuals gather and participate in ceremonies, after which there is a feast. Considering my age, I was granted only one day of fasting. However, I told the healer that I had previously fasted for seven days, consuming nothing but water as part of a Jain ritual. He yielded to my wish and granted four days of fasting. We travelled by car 1600 kilometres north of Toronto to an area near James Bay, Quebec. Upon arrival, the very next day, we were taken into the wilderness, given tents, sleeping bags, etc. As an elderly person, I was allowed to have a bottle of water for my medicines. We were placed at some distance from each other and did not know the whereabouts of the others. The only people who visited us twice a day to make sure we were safe and well were those who tended to the sacred fire at the main base. We were to meditate or reflect about our life all day. At night it got quite cold. Following the four days of fasting, we were taken back to the main campsite where the sacred fire was burning. Four of us who had fasted sat around the fire with the healer and his helpers and described our fasting experience including visions we had received. After this there were a drumming and singing ceremony and a buffet dinner. I found it interesting that before we were allowed to serve ourselves, one of the healer's helpers made a ceremonial food plate, took it outside, and put it under a nearby tree. This was an offering to spirits who had helped fasting individuals with the vision quests. Having a sacred fire, a vision quest, and fasting in the wilderness followed by celebration and offerings to the spirits reminded me a lot of my ancient Hindu culture.

You may ask did I receive a vision during my fast? On our way from

Toronto to Chisasibi, we had heard that the federal government had declared June 21 as National Indigenous Day. During my fast, I contemplated about many things in my life including the Indigenous situation in Canada. I realized that many Canadians were still ignorant about it and needed to be educated. I came with the vision that we should celebrate the newly proclaimed Indigenous Day with a forum in which we highlighted injustices suffered by the Indigenous peoples of Canada. The day's focus would be the broken Kelowna Accord, an agreement signed by all provinces, territories, national Indigenous organizations, and the federal government in November 2005 under the Liberal leadership of Prime Minister Paul Martin. Following the loss of the election in January 2006 by Mr Martin, the Right Honorable Steven Harper, Conservative Prime Minister, negated the accord.

Upon return from fasting, I decided to implement my vision and organized a forum, *The Broken Promises in Promised Land*. I considered it appropriate to invite Paul Martin as a keynote speaker. I approached his office to invite him and initially was told he was already booked for that day for a function in Winnipeg. No doubt, I was disappointed. But to my surprise, I received a phone call from his office the next day, and they said Mr Martin had accepted my invitation and had rescheduled his event in Winnipeg. The event was successful and attended by over 400 people, and was reported by various news organization.

Public Protests

With the recent death of George Floyd, there have been huge protests across the globe. This and similar events such as shootings in schools and attacks on synagogues and mosques have drawn a large amount of sympathy and compassion from people. However, much of the sympathy is, if I may give an honest opinion, of the moment, opportunistic, or pretence on the part of politicians that they are doing something. Mass protests and social media exposure for an issue are necessary to attract public attention. However, sustained commitment is needed to bring about social change.

I am not against public protest. In my time I have marched too. For the first time in my life, at the age of sixty-seven, I participated in a protest march against the American invasion of Iraq in 2003. I walked carrying a placard in front of the United States consulate in downtown Toronto with a group of people unknown to me; somehow, it was a liberating experience to know I had done my civic duty. However, did I continue my involvement in the movement? I am sorry to say I did not. The second protest march I was involved in was related to the Government's reducing of the welfare rate in Ontario. With two other like-minded physicians in their white coats, we walked two kilometres along with many welfare recipients, social activists, and others from the Metropolitan United Church to the legislative building. This was a cause for which I had already shown a life-long commitment. I consider joining a protest march for a cause you believe in to be a civic act, which signifies dissent against unjust policies and actions, a form of civil disobedience.

11

Moving the Titanic: Fighting Systemic Racism Visible Minorities at the University of Toronto

> When you get these jobs that you have been so brilliantly trained for, just remember that your real job is that if you are free, you need to free somebody else. If you have some power, then your job is to empower somebody else. This is not just a grab-bag candy game.
>
> TONI MORRISON

There are many things that we somehow fail to notice when we get busy with our routine life. Most of us focus on finishing our work and tackling the highs and lows that come with every job. But what we usually end up forgetting is the power that lies within our hands. It may not be too much, but it could be enough to touch another life. Furthermore, one is filled with lots of self-doubt when trying to change entrenched policies of very large public funded institutions with annual budget of over one billion dollars. However, with persistence and coalition of similar minded individuals, it is possible to change the so called "unmovable." In 1999, just when my retirement was looming, I suddenly looked up and noticed the lack of visible minority faculty members in my department. Only one other person was from a visible minority.

Under the Canadian Federal Employment Equity Act 1995,

visible minorities are defined as persons other than Indigenous people, who are non-Caucasian in race or not white in colour. I was scheduled to retire in 2001 and my Chinese colleague John Hsieh in 2003, leaving behind a completely white faculty. This did not reflect the multicultural nature of the student body or the City of Toronto, of which visible minorities constituted 57 percent and 37 percent respectively. At the time, the department was undertaking strategic planning for the next five years. As an associate chair, I was a member of several committees that analyzed the department's future. I consistently attempted to discuss the importance of faculty diversity, but these went unheard. Because of my conventional education and the years of experience that have made me who I am, I always believed that public health practitioners are much more aware of social justice and equity; but it seemed that this belief was hardly evident when it came to the makeup of our faculty.

I had developed a sound understanding of Canada's diversity issues. Since its inception, Canada has had a long history of racial discrimination, originally against Indigenous and Black people, and then the Chinese, Japanese South Asian, Jewish, and other people, including Ukrainians. In 1962, Canada ended racial discrimination as a feature of its immigration system. In 1967 a point system was introduced to rank potential immigrants for eligibility. This resulted in an influx of immigrants from almost everywhere on the globe, giving the country a multicultural demographic. However, despite this infusion of many cultures, many Canadians were still accustomed to white Canadian, especially Anglo and French, dominance.

Many new visible minority Canadians faced discrimination because of their skin colour and cultural heritage. Mainstream white Canadians often overlooked their achievements in education or career experiences in their home countries. Few visible minorities could return to school or overcome hurdles by taking extra training or the multitude of licensing examinations to gain the necessary qualifications that seemed to be there only to obstruct them. This systemic discrimination resulted in the white homogeneity of experience-intensive careers within the University of Toronto's faculty. Some few visible minorities had managed to overcome these obstacles and gain entrance into faculty positions, but these were exceptions and, while racial and cultural diversity in Canadian workplaces was increasing, it was at an incredibly sluggish rate.

There was a steady increase in the number of visible minorities attending post-secondary education in Canada, often the children of first-generation immigrants whose parents were professionals. These new Canadians valued and understood the importance of higher education much more than many white Canadians who had immigrated earlier as trade persons or labourers. The reason for this was that when Canada opened its borders to non-Europeans in 1962, its point system admitted mainly highly educated professionals such as doctors and engineers from developing countries. The increased amount of visible minority professionals seemed to indicate that Canada's white homogeneity in the upper echelons of the workplace was beginning to crumble. Diversity in the workplace seemed to be on the way to becoming a recognized fact of Canadian life.

Sadly, racial prejudice continued to rear its ugly face, as many white Canadians continued to cling to their perceived superiority. This often led to white individuals with the same qualifications as their visible minority peers finding favour with employers. As a professor and associate chair of the Department of Public Health Sciences, I was determined to make sure that the department installed measures to combat such discriminatory practices and encourage diversity.

I began my diversity campaign with an open letter to all faculty members and graduate students:

Dear colleagues and graduate students

I have one major concern, which I thought would surface at our retreat or search committees but did not. I know all of us are committed to the principles of social justice, equity, and racial diversity. However, unless we become sensitive to racial diversity in our search process, this department will become "colourless" when Prof John Hsieh leaves us in June 2003. At this time, at least half the City of Toronto's population will be peoples of colour. Professor Harvey Skinner had on his door a statement which said something to the effect that silence is not always golden, and for the sake of social justice, we must break the silence. I hope you will all forgive me for breaking the silence . . .

If we truly believe that publicly funded institutions like ours should reflect the society we live in and that we are really committed to diversity and social justice, then we must seize this window of opportunity to act. Advocacy must begin at home, and we should walk the talk. Once these search processes are finished, we will have colleagues who will hopefully be with us for the next 15 to 25 years. This proactive step will also help the department recruit bright and young students from different racial groups, better its relationship with its alumni, and raise funds from the community and alumni . . .

I hope we collectively chart a course of which we all could be proud. If you feel this issue deserves attention, please write to our Chair and, if you wish, I shall be happy to receive a copy of your email. Thank you for your kind attention.

To my relief, I found an unexpected number of supporters among my peers and the graduate students, who wrote to the Chair about the need for an inclusive faculty. Some graduate students even indicated that they would not consider continuing to work with the department in the future unless the department became inclusive. The response was overwhelming. It also made me ponder over the power of taking an initiative. At the beginning of what seems to be a challenge, one might think one is the sole warrior. But it's when you take an initiative and present a chance to others that you realize that there are people out there who would be happy to be part of your battle. All they need is a little nudge.

The Chair of the Department of Public Health Sciences (now known as the Dalla Lana School of Public Health or DLSPH) Dr Harvey Skinner was startled to receive many emails. I had a very close relationship with him, as he always addressed me as "father." Feeling hurt, he asked why I had not approached him before sending the email. I told him of four instances when I had tried to broach this subject. He then set up a task force to address the issue. I was asked to be the chair of the task force, but declined, as I understood that the faculty who would work beyond my retirement would have to live with the task force's decisions.

The chair established the task force in May 1999; a committee was constituted to include representation from white and non-white faculty and students and an individual from the community, and chaired jointly by a faculty member Dr Blake Poland and senior graduate student Elaine Power. The task force met five times that May and June, and continued deliberations via email throughout July.

The long-term vision for the Department of Public Health Sciences concerning issues of diversity was to have a minimum of fifteen percent of its tenure-track faculty from identified visible minorities and Indigenous Peoples (since within the Canadian population, the composition of the visible minority and Indigenous people at that time was fifteen percent). This would be linked to developing a student body that reflected the community's ethnoracial diversity as closely as possible. Some of the community, such as Black and Indigenous students, were underrepresented. In such a situation, a summer mentorship program for these students would be set up, as had been done in the Faculty of Medicine.

Race, ethnicity and culture are important social determinants of health. All of us strongly felt that bringing this much-needed change would help decrease health gaps and achieve health equity.

From the River to the Ocean . . .

The warmth with which my department embraced my suggestions regarding the hiring of visible minorities prompted me to broaden my target. A thorough analysis of the current University of Toronto faculty was in order. I was interested in addressing the future of diversity in the university as a whole.

At this time, the University of Toronto was under public scrutiny after a Chinese Professor, Kin-Yip Chun, in the Faculty of Engineering, was denied tenure. He had accused the University of racism in their decision. A social-minded law professor, Professor Peter Russell, and a dedicated activist student body took up his case. I was asked to join their group, but I declined because I believed that their group was too focussed on an individual case, whereas I was trying to address the systemic nature of racism. It seemed to me that if the university had different groups pressuring it on the same issue, the outcome would be better. In September 1986, many Canadian universities, including the University of Toronto, became signatories to the Federal Contractors Program, which allows the university to bid on federal contracts over $200,000. In becoming a participant, the University of Toronto certified its commitment to implement employment equity, following eleven criteria, and agreeing to a clause that clearly stated that the university must comply with the "establishment of goals and timetables for the hiring, training and promotion of the designated group employees."

Using available data, I studied the university's entire faculty composition, noting the number of visible minorities. I discovered that in 1990, 9.4 percent of the faculty members were self-identified visible minorities whereas, in 1999 the representation had fallen to 8.7 percent despite University of Toronto President Robert S Pritchard's pledge to increase diversity in his inaugural speech in 1990.

The president's office knew me well. Armed with all the necessary information, I called the president's executive assistant, Kashinath Rao (a fellow of South Asian decent), for a meeting to discuss the University's lack of diversity. During our long meeting, he tried to assure me that the university was taking all the necessary steps—he believed my concerns were unwarranted. At the end of the meeting, I handed him approximately thirty emails I had received from colleagues in my department that discussed their unease with the university's lack of diversity. As politely as possible, I asked him to take off his rose-tinted glasses and left the room. I left with a heavy heart in the belief that I hadn't made much of an impact on Mr Rao.

To my pleasant surprise, he called me the next morning acknowledging my concerns and recommended that I speak to the provost, who dealt with academic and faculty matters. My heart did a hundred happy somersaults; but then I remembered how the university worked. From flying high, in a moment I forced myself to land on solid ground with a thud! I told him it would take a long time to receive an appointment with the provost. He immediately assuaged my fears and said he would facilitate the appointment for the very next day.

During my meeting with the Provost, Adel Sedra, I again outlined my concerns about the lack of the university's diversity. He gave me the impression that he was unconvinced, and tried to reassure me that I had no reason to worry; he believed the university was doing all it could. He asked me to have patience. He was an Egyptian and he reminded me how difficult it was to find samosas in Canada in the past when we had to travel considerable distances to get them. Now it was available in nearby grocery stores.

My excitement of the previous day was thus short-lived. I was disappointed for being unable to convince the provost of the alarming nature of the university faculty's disproportionate composition. This was especially disappointing because of President Prichard's pledge of 1990 to address issues of ethno-racial inequity:

> The university should establish a policy that encourages prospective faculty members from visible minorities to apply, and that gives them a fair chance of being selected. This would involve broadening the curriculum to encompass subjects of interest to a wide range of people, making search committees accountable for advertising positions in such a way that qualified members of minorities are located and encouraged to apply, making search committees aware that qualified candidates of all ethnic backgrounds must be given fair consideration, and the search committees should report on the disposition of candidates from ethnic minorities for all appointments. If candidates are equal academically, the candidate from a minority background and/or a woman should be given a bonus on the hiring grid.

It seemed as though it was quite easy for people to write what was politically correct and expected, but the reality was starkly different. Even when I was chair of the Faculty Council in the Faculty of Medicine from 1995 to 1998, I had never seen any implementation of these recommendations—at no point were the recommendations ever considered during faculty hiring or curriculum creation. This major problem was compounded by the fact that important events that profoundly impacted faculty composition were beginning to transpire. In 1999, the provost's office had announced that the university would be hiring 100 new professors per year for the next five years. Prime Minister Jean Chrétien promised that the Canadian government would support approximately 2000 new research chairs in universities over a few years after 1999; the University of Toronto was likely to get a further 200 to 250 of these new academic positions. It would be hiring approximately 750 new professors from 1999 to 2004. At the time, I could see that such hiring would have a significant impact on the ethno-racial composition of the faculty for many years to come; once appointed to a job, most individuals stay at the job for a minimum of thirty years. As mentioned above, my meeting with the provost led me to believe that faculty diversity was not on the administrative agenda. The annual budget of the University of Toronto in 2000 was over one billion dollars and to influence such a powerful institution was equal to moving the Titanic! I was not sure I would be the right person to do this. Yes, yes, I too have my moments of self-doubt. No matter how many successful battles one fights, self-doubt manages to rear its ugly head occasionally.

For a while I was lost. I had no strategy. I was troubled. After a few months, it became clear that I must back my plea with concrete evidence. Academia always believes that decisions are supposed to be evidence-based. It occurred to me that the University of Toronto prides itself as a national university. If that was so, its faculty must, at a minimum, have minority representation that exists at the national demographic level. In 2000, fifteen percent of the population was visible minority and Indigenous combined; hence, the faculty should target a fifteen percent visible minority composition.

The Psychological Association in the United States of America had also published at the time that meaningful representations of visible minorities in organizations must have a critical mass of fifteen percent. My brain began ticking away. A delicious challenge awaited me!

Working with a graduate student, Tomislav Svoboda, I began to construct a mathematical model that would use past trends in diversity, such as the number of visible minorities hired per year or the visible minority turnover rate, to approximate the future composition of the university faculty in terms of diversity.

Upon the complete development of our model, it became clear that the results were so alarming that there was no conceivable way the university would not be forced to act. Using our simulation model and a "minimal" hiring practice where fifteen percent of recruits from visible minorities was an approachable goal rather than a quota, we found that it would take somewhere between 25 and 119 years to reach the desired minority rate of fifteen percent. I could scarcely believe these results. I would not have believed that the faculty composition issue at the university was so ridiculously out of hand. While I would have preferred to present my findings to the president, his office seemed to show little interest in my cause. This was also around the time when the University of Toronto was recruiting its new president. I wanted to make sure that the new president understood diversity and would be committed to addressing the issue in a meaningful manner. Because of this, I felt that garnering a large amount of public support would best suit my cause.

Helen Keller had once said, "Alone, we can do so little; together, we can do so much." Taking inspiration from this famous quote, I decided to get all hands on board. First, I approached *Bulletin*, University of Toronto's weekly newspaper, and *Toronto Star*, a newspaper with extensive circulation. I prepared a report on our motivation, findings, and what we hoped to achieve. The article was published in both *Bulletin* and *Toronto Star* on 10 January 2000. The trend in diversity growth at the university from 2000 to 2060 is shown below.

Projected Proportion of Faculty Who are from a Visible Minority at the University of Toronto

[Where each year15% of new faculty are from a Visible Minority]

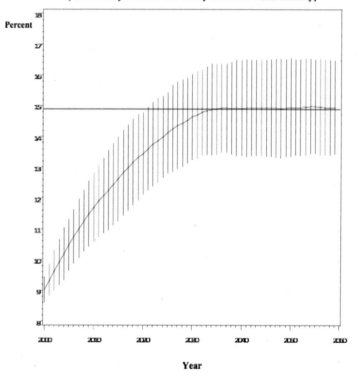

Note: 1) solid curve indicates the average proportion of faculty who are from a visible minority in each year
2) The vertical lines indicate the 95% confidence interval for each year
3) The plot is based on an average of results from 200 simulations of a 100 year projection
4) Current faculty age distribution is taken into account and the age distribution of new hirees is right skewed with a mean of 27.

These published articles generated widespread publicity. The *Toronto Star* headline on 10 January 2000 read, Visible Minorities Not Visible at U of T.

I was overwhelmed by the interview requests from print, radio, and television media, both mainstream and community based. A few negative comments about reverse discrimination also came my way. This is one malicious letter I received:

January 12th, 2000

Prof. Dr Chandrakant Shah
University of Toronto
Dept of Public Health Sciences

Professor Chandrakant Shah,

So you came to this country, this Canada, from some other country, India. Don't come here and call us names because you feel we're not being sensitive to your "diversity". Screw your diversity. Either come here to be like us—because you come to our country, we didn't go to your screwed-up country—or get yourself gone. It is not we who should change to make you feel comfortable. You are the one who must change and be sensitive to us. You're the guest. Not us. Live by our rules, or beat it. And if you sneaked into this country illegally, then you'd better get your ass out of here and apply through legal means. And if you can't, then that's just the way it'll have to be. You don't have a right to be in this country unless WE say you can be here. Period.

This is our country. We built it. We will decide how it's run. We'll decide who can join us as citizens. We speak English here. We do things in certain ways. That's our choice and it's not your right to come here to tell us that we have to be more like you. We don't want to be like you and we don't want our country to be like your old country.

Flavius Janus

While the cause I was standing up for received widespread attention and media coverage, there were things to be sorted out on the personal front. When the articles in *Bulletin* and *Toronto Star* came out, I felt that it was only right to go and reconcile with President Prichard, who was bound to be unhappy with the massive amount of negative publicity that the University of Toronto received. I sent him a letter to clarify my intentions and asked for his forgiveness so that we could, together, create a better future for the university.

President Prichard's term at the university was ending, and the university soon announced that Dr Robert Birgeneau would be replacing him in July 2000.

At the same time the Faculty of Medicine's seat on the governing council had recently vacated, and a new member of my faculty had to be elected to fill it. Realizing that the best way to get the voices of the pro-diversity movement heard was to gain a seat at the governing table, which decided such university-wide issues, I put forth my name for the upcoming election. No doubt, I was nervous as I was going to be competing against a well-known senior scientist whom I admired. Even though I couldn't see myself winning in my wildest dreams, to my shock and to the surprise of many others, I was elected a member of the governing council on 1 July 2000. I felt that now it would be much easier to push forward the diversity issue. In October, my group made a presentation to the governing council, which was a large step. It greatly increased the force of the governing council to address the lack of faculty diversity.

The diversity campaign faced major challenges. Many people dismissed our message as unimportant and were largely apathetic. Therefore it was hard to show the governing council that a large number of people did support us. It occurred to me that an event where supporters could express their concerns would be useful for the cause. I dismissed the idea of a protest march in the belief that it would be better to take a more conciliatory approach. Thus was born the Diversity Celebration.

The United Nations had proclaimed March 21 as a Day of Elimination of Racial Discrimination. This day would surely make a perfect backdrop for our pro-diversity message. We planned to invite administrators, faculty, and students from all ethnic groups to collectively celebrate this day and showcase some of the successes different faculties had achieved in fighting racism within the university and highlight the importance of diversity. Also, we intended to invite some high-ranking community leaders from Toronto to speak. I proposed a gathering at the university's Convocation Hall, where we would celebrate and commend the president's office for promoting diversity and its ongoing efforts for the cause. The hall held approximately 1700 people and was an ambitious venue to use. I invited the recently appointed president to speak about the university's progress in fighting racism and improving diversity, encouraging him to announce his office's goals and their proposed timetable, both of which were required by the Governing Council Policy document of 28 March 1991. We hoped to inspire the president to develop definite plans for encouraging diversity, proving to the community that the university was committed to employment equity.

In addition to the president, we invited R Roy McMurtry, the Chief Justice of Ontario, who was well known for his support in the fight against racism, and Zanana Akande, a former minister of Ontario's Provincial Parliament and a woman of colour, to speak. The Mayor of Toronto's office sent a representative. Also present was Senator Vivienne Poy whose office had supported my cause and who was appointed Chancellor of the University of Toronto in 2004. All the eminences extolled the diverse composition of the city and the importance of tolerance. The atmosphere was electrifying.

Finally, President Birgeneau spoke and explained his perception of diversity at the University, concluding by outlining the steps he intended to take, namely: i) all new searches would be proactive in hiring minorities, including international candidates, Indigenous persons, persons with disabilities, and women where they were underrepresented; he rejected the concept of a quota for any group; ii) once appointed, younger new members would be mentored for leadership positions; iii) appointment of an employment equity consultant to develop appropriate policies and practices; and iv) appointment of a new vice-president of Human Resources, with a strengthened mandate for employment equity.

Over 700 people attended the event, much greater than the 400 attendees I had predicted. The president's office hosted an informal luncheon reception following the event, having planned for no more than 250 people, and it was embarrassing that we ran out of food!

It was obviously hard for the University of Toronto to accept the systemic problems lurking in its structure. But when it did, it rose to the challenge admirably. In 2020, long after I had retired, I came across its annual report on employment equity. Now 21.9 percent of the surveyed faculty members identified themselves as visible minorities. Changing the employment policies at the largest Canadian university with its annual budget of over one billion dollars was like changing the direction of the Titanic! It needed evidence, mobilization, and sheer persistence. I was a part of this. Despite the self-doubt and helplessness I had felt at the initial stage of this journey, I felt humbled and quietly smiled to myself.

However, as they say, "the wicked witch has no rest." Working in the field of diversity and equity, my eyes automatically scan for diversity in the workplace. You may call it hypervigilance or paranoia; to me, it is who I have evolved to be. In January 2019, I was looking for the contact information of a former colleague at the website of the Canadian Blood Services (CBS). I knew he would be listed in their upper management. What I saw shocked me. There was a complete lack of diverse representation in the board and executive. The CBS is a charitable corporation funded totally by Canadian taxpayers with an annual budget of $1.2 billion. It was running right under the watchful eyes of the ministers of health of all the territories and provinces except Quebec, who happen to be responsible for appointing board members. CBS collects blood and plasma from volunteers and distributes these and blood products to hospitals and clinics across Canada except Quebec.

Following my observation, I started a one-person letter-writing campaign, bringing to the attention of the board their lack of representation and inclusion. While the board acknowledged the situation and said they had been working on a plan to rectify the situation since 2017, they were unable to provide any action plan. There was none. Over the next two years, I ended up writings several times to their board and corporate board members and presented a petition to the board with more than 1000 signatures, and endorsement letters from the mayors of a few of Canada's largest municipalities, and members of parliament and provincial legislatures. I also wrote letters to the editors of large newspapers, which never saw the light of day. I felt completely ignored and desperate, ready to give up. As a last measure, in late September 2021, finally I requested to their board to present a brief at their public meeting in December 2021. To my amazement, just two weeks prior to the public meeting, their Chief Executive Officer, Dr Graham Sher released a video statement on their website admitting the existence of systemic racism at CBS and promising to rectify the situation. To date, CBS has made some progress: twenty-five percent of the board members and eighteen percent of the EMTs are from racialized minorities, including one Indigenous board member. It was an arduous journey particularly for an octogenarian like me, but in the end, the result was well worth it.

12

Advocating for Children

As a doctor who deals with patients from different backgrounds, cultures, and ages, one tends to end up observing more than the symptoms of a health issue. Patients talk. I listen. Every day is a new experience and every conversation food for thought. I am sure there are many who diagnose the problem, write the prescription, and move on to the next patient. But somehow the paths my mind travelled on have always been different, always longer . . . always on the search for something more. Being aware of the impact of social determinants such as income, education, employment status, culture, and race on the state of health, access to health care and health outcomes, I always treated the *person* with the health problem, and not the problem by itself. I treated my marginalized clients with empathy. But I knew they needed more than what I could give. To be physically and emotionally healthy, they needed adequate income, steady employment, a healthy diet, and shelter. When sick, they needed more than medical care.

While our society has provided a fair amount of assistance through its various welfare programs, those are minimal at best and usually lag behind inflation. From time to time, depending upon the political party in power, there are cutbacks or, occasionally, marginal augmentations. Depending on the nature of the illness, a few receive help from voluntary and charitable organizations. On the other hand, researchers who study the impact of social determinants on health merely publish a paper or report and expect policymakers or social activists to take necessary actions, which often doesn't happen by itself. I decided that I would not be just a bystander. I wanted to be an advocate for change. Where this impulse came about in me to act, I don't know. I was not this way in India, which does not lack problems. In Canada injustice has always pulled me to act, to try and do something. I would bring my status as a professor and my professional skills to effect change. Idle no more! I told myself. Fortunately, in the last five years I have witnessed changes in attitude, where physicians write prescriptions for the homeless and the destitute with recommendations such as "needs a home," "adequate and nutritious diet," and "income supplement" instead of a list of medications and tests.

As mentioned before, I was an iterant physician in remote and isolated Indigenous communities in the Sioux Lookout Zone in northern Ontario. In 1985, I visited Bear Skin Lake First Nations Community, situated 50° north and 90° west, 425 kilometres north of Sioux Lookout. It had an approximate population of 500 and was accessible only by air in the summer and the "winter road." Once there, I was asked to make a home visit by canoe to a woman who lived on the other side of a lake.

A single mother, she had multiple sclerosis and struggled greatly with mobility and other daily activities. She had four children, all under the age of twelve. She told me that her major problem was not her own health, but that her children were starving. Her pantry was empty. I was truly shaken. In our own backyard, I thought, people were starving in our Canada! How ironical, and Canada one of the breadbaskets of the world!

To digress, in 2004, a graduate student at the Ontario Institute of Studies in Education had undertaken a doctoral dissertation on "teaching of spirituality" in professional school courses such as medicine, social work, and nursing, other than in theology departments. As part of his thesis, he interviewed a few professors, including me, since I was known for my research on the impact of spirituality on health. He asked me, "Do you recall a moment or incident when you had some epiphany?" I bluntly told him no. He kept insisting that I try to recall such an event, as all other professors interviewed by him had such a moment leading them to include spirituality in their courses. I explained to him that all my work was guided by a notion that "if it is the good thing to do, do it." Later, in retrospect, I felt the incident of that home visit to that single mother was indeed my epiphany. I was galvanized. That was when I knew I could no longer observe unmoved, I had to act!

When I returned to Toronto, one of my priorities thenceforth was to work to improve the conditions of our vulnerable children, more specifically to eliminate poverty. Poverty needs to be addressed as a social determinant of health and not only as a social problem. For my voice to be heard, I needed support from the powerful, rich, and influential. The collective voice of physicians would influence my cause. I was a member of the Child Welfare Committee of the Ontario Medical Association (OMA). The OMA has a membership of about 16,000 licensed physicians. One of their mandates is to advocate for the health of the population of Ontario.

I approached the Committee and requested that we advocate for children living in poverty. While it was easy to convince the committee members, it was not easy to sway the higher powers within the OMA to release resources. I argued that if the public perceived that the OMA truly cared for poor people, that would help their image. It would also help when they negotiated their fees with the government. That worked. We began by reviewing the existing medical literature in Canada and abroad, including the famous Black Report in the United Kingdom, "Inequalities in Health: Report of a Research Working Group," published in August 1980. The group found that there were differences in mortality rates across social groups, with those in lower social groups suffering higher rates of mortality. We discovered that a large body of work confirmed the negative effects of poor socioeconomic standing on children's health, in particular, poor living conditions are associated with chronic disabilities, sickness, and premature deaths.

Fortunately, the timing was perfect, as in 1986 the Government of Ontario was undertaking a review of its social assistance programs. A large percentage of people on social assistance were parents responsible for their children's wellbeing. The review commission held public hearings. Under the banner of OMA, I, on behalf of the Child Welfare Committee, presented a brief outlining the impact of poor living conditions on children's health. We also made a presentation to the City of Toronto's Social Welfare Department. These generated a good amount of attention.

I received an interesting two-page handwritten letter from a grandmother who was visiting from Nova Scotia and had read about my report in a local newspaper. She wrote to me about her son, who was very poor and lived on social assistance with his wife and four children under six years. She told me about how he was forced to leave his kids at home when he went grocery shopping because they asked for things they couldn't afford. She assured me that while they were not starving, they did not have many things which other children in the community had. She challenged me to do something about it beyond writing a report and presenting a brief. I understood her anguish; however, I could not do much except sensitize the public and policymakers by presenting evidence and swaying public opinion and policymakers to formulate healthy public policies. We could also sensitize health care professionals to consider poverty as one of the major factors influencing their patients' health in their clinical encounters. It is heart-warming to see that this is finally happening, and the Canadian College of Family Physicians is channelling its efforts into primary care curricula.

To sensitize practicing physicians, my colleagues and I published a paper on our findings in the Canadian Medical Association Journal. Following this, we presented a brief to the Senate Committee's Hearing on Children, providing the health dimension to their discussion on children living in poverty. In 1990, Ed Broadbent, the federal New Democratic Party (NDP) leader at the time, was retiring. He had been a champion for the elimination of child poverty and had earned a great deal of goodwill all around. When he proposed a final resolution to eliminate child poverty by 2000 in Canada, the parliament passed the bill unanimously. Unfortunately, that promise has not been fulfilled so far; but successive federal governments have reduced the number of children living in poverty with their child credit and other support programs. A slow incremental gain, indeed, an evolutionary feature of social change!

Another area of concern regarding vulnerable children is the foster home situation.

During my residency in 1963 at Chicago's St Vincent's Orphanage, I provided primary care for over 100 children aged six months to five years. Catholic nuns ran the orphanage and the only other persons working there were a maintenance man and me; the children used to call us "mommy" as they didn't know the difference between men and women. Having seen the conditions of these children and also realizing the very privileged position that I was blessed to be in, I seriously considered adopting a needy child but respected my wife's decision to have our own.

As mentioned earlier, in the fall of 1970 I took up a new job at the Children's Aid Society of Vancouver. The commonly held view amongst pediatricians was that only old and tired pediatricians worked at the CAS and that it was not a place for a young and energetic man at the beginning of his career. However, I always believed that it was up to an individual to make the work exciting. During my short tenure at CAS, I was often in the news appealing on behalf of the children's cause. Previously, the children coming into the care of Children's Aid Society in Canada were infants whose unwed mothers had decided to give them up for adoption. With the easing of the abortion laws and the availability of birth control pills in the 1960s, the situation had changed. Now, many children coming into care were from difficult family situations or having chronic health problems. With the change in the Juvenile Delinquent Act, youths under eighteen were diverted by the courts to the Children's Aid Society instead of juvenile detention centres. Many of these youths suffered from emotional and behavioural disorders. Many disabled children were also admitted to CAS due to their parents' inability to cope physically or financially.

I had not anticipated encountering so many children with disabilities and was perplexed as to whether this was a phenomenon only in Vancouver—or was this was a condition prevalent throughout British Columbia. It led me to apply and receive a grant to study the prevalence of chronic handicaps in child-welfare care. It was an arduous task to manage a full-time practice and a province-wide study. However, it was completed, and we concluded that forty percent of all children in care had physical, developmental, or emotional handicaps, and half of them were severely handicapped. This result made headlines across the nation.

While I was making progress in leaps and bounds in my

profession, on the home front, things were not at all easy. My two young children, who were both under three, was cared for by Sudha single-handedly. This was difficult, especially because of my regular absence. But Sudha turned out to be the wind beneath my wings— she was extremely understanding and managed well. My twenty-two-year-old younger brother had just arrived in Vancouver and was living with us; his presence and help made her life a little easier.

The care for children at the community level called for dedicated foster- or group-home parents with appropriate training, especially in helping children with disabilities. It was not always easy to recruit foster- or group-home parents. Many of them lacked experience, and quite a few complained about receiving inadequate remuneration. All these factors led to frequent placement breakdowns requiring moving children to other homes. Those with emotional problems often went through a revolving-door phenomenon, i.e., having to move to several different homes in a relatively short period.

An eight-year-old boy admitted to the hospital for a minor surgery came with a bag containing all his belongings, for he was unsure if his present foster parents would take him back. At this tender age he had felt unwanted and was prepared for yet another move. He had lived in twenty-one different homes in the previous two years.

Many families signed up to become foster parents to augment their income, while others for altruism or genuine love for children. No doubt, the agency screened prospective volunteers by visiting their homes and checking their backgrounds before accepting them. However, this was not always so.

The majority of the foster parents were wonderful and caring people, and a lifeline for these children. But to encourage and retain their services, adequate remuneration had to be provided. They were paid the rate set by the agency for caring for children without any disabilities. There were no defined rates for care for disabled children; it was left to the discretion of the individual social worker assigned to the case, and varied depending on the workers' experience, seniority, and ability to deploy the system. It also depended on how strongly the foster family made their case for an increase in their compensation. As a medical director, I was frequently consulted by the workers to gauge the intensity of care required for such a child, and also received pleas from foster parents to discuss with their social worker the difficulties they encountered in caring for these children. I started noticing that those foster parents with the ability to convince workers received higher compensations than those who remained silent. In essence, those with the louder voice received the greater reward!

This situation led me to conclude that:

1. When these children were placed in foster care, the foster parents needed a realistic picture about the severity of handicaps and the extra efforts that would be required. A care plan was needed based on the child's need when admitted, to be reviewed periodically. This would prevent breakdowns in placement, thus reducing the emotional trauma associated with frequent moves.

2. To determine a foster family's board rates, the agency should develop an objective instrument based on the child's age and the care needed, with consideration for a child with disabilities.

I initially proposed the idea in an article in the *Child Welfare Journal*. Subsequently, I set out to develop an actionable plan. I was assisted in this effort by my social work colleague, Susan Pulose, Director of Research at the agency, and others. Our first task was to develop the definition of handicap and the efforts required for the foster parents to care for such a child. Depending on the type of disability, we defined five categories of care: personal care, supervision of medical care, therapeutic physical care, ancillary care and therapeutic emotional care. The most challenging task was specifying therapeutic emotional care, which initially had focused on specific emotional or behavioural problems presented by the children (a list of sixty), and later was redefined to encompass "parenting behaviour" required by the child as a result of his emotional handicap. We finally developed a field test with social workers and foster parents on a reliable and valid scale that would be objective.

Following this rigorous development work, we published our results in *Child Welfare Journal*. To our surprise, within a short period after publication, I received letters asking permission to reproduce and use it widely from Kansas and Arkansas, Florida and New York City, Israel, England, New Zealand. It was immensely gratifying to learn that our work had wide-scale appeal and would hopefully bring relief for the foster parents caring for children with disabilities.

13

Equity and Social Justice in Other Areas

In this account of my struggles of what I perceived as injustices and lack of fair play that worked against the philosophy of multiculturalism and diversity, of which this country is proud, I hope I don't come across as merely a troublemaker looking out for causes, portraying myself as a David fighting many Goliaths. But I have lived a long life, and we live in a complex, evolving society, and as a public health specialist I see it as my duty to point out problems as I saw them from that perspective. Let me list now other areas of concern.

Unemployment and Health

> Let's destroy the myth that unemployment is free, that there's no cost to people being unemployed or living in poverty. It's a huge cost in human terms, and a financial cost to our society.
>
> AUDREY MCLAUGHLIN, LEADER OF THE NDP, 1989–1995

In 1993, I attended the Ninth International Congress on Circumpolar Health in Reykjavik, Iceland. At the time, Iceland was going through a terrible recession. During the conference, I heard my Icelandic colleagues' grave concern about their high unemployment rate and its consequences on their people. This concern was echoed extensively in their media. That was when I became curious about the rate of unemployment. What I discovered was truly astonishing. Historically, the unemployment rate in Iceland has been around 2.4 percent to 2.8 percent! Many people in Iceland had part-time jobs over and above their full-time ones to meet the high cost of living, attributed to importing most common goods from other countries. During the recession of 1993, the unemployment rate rose to 4.8 percent, and all part-time jobs almost disappeared, which resulted in an enormous strain on individual families to make ends meet. The government and social agencies had initiated major changes to abate its effect by making it easy to access programs of income subsidies, social housing, child protection, and food distribution.

I began to think about my homeland, Canada, where the unemployment rate was a shocking 12 percent to 13 percent. While there were discussions about its social cost at the political level, including those raised by social agencies, the health sector was completely silent. Historically, Canada's unemployment level has been around 5.6 percent to 6.0 percent. The impact of social determinants such as poverty, unemployment, and homelessness on health receives minimum attention in medical curricula; while it would be intuitive, many of us had little knowledge about the extent to which unemployment affected health in general and mental health in particular. Upon my return to Canada, I decided that I must try and find out more.

At that time I was a member of the Population Health Committee of the Ontario Medical Association (OMA). I proposed to the committee that we undertake the task of studying the serious impact of unemployment on national health and what we could do to help as health professionals. I was fortunate that one committee member, the OMA health policy director Carol Jacobson, also my former student, among others was extremely supportive of the initiative and quickly approved a small budget to get the work started.

I was keenly aware that social and welfare workers and activists were already telling tragic stories about unemployed people. I thought our advocacy work should provide extra ammunition to make their case stronger. Our committee decided that our first task would be to hire a physician specializing in public health to study the empirical evidence on how unemployment impacts national health and estimate the extra health care costs to the nation. We were fortunate to recruit the late Dr Robert Jin who was working as a part-time medical consultant with the Ontario Ministry of Labour and was my former student.

One vitally important economic and social (and indeed cultural and political) determinant of people's health is work, especially employment. In modern society, employment means steady work for which money is received. The necessity of earning money for daily survival (and preferably a decent standard of living) makes paid employment often the top priority in most people's lives. For these reasons, work can significantly influence people's mental, physical, and social health. There is plenty of research and empirical evidence on the health effects of different jobs and workplace settings. Epidemiological evidence, such as the renowned Whitehall study of British civil servants, has shown how workplace organizations' hierarchy significantly impacts health outcomes (including mortality)—the people in the lowest-status jobs (with the least sense of control) having the worst outcomes. Job satisfaction is also an important determinant of health.

Of course, people perform work such as childcare, household chores, and voluntary work in the community without receiving pay. However, employment is generally more highly valued by individuals and society, and not only because it provides needed income. For many people, employment provides a sense of regularity, purpose, and identity; social status and social connectedness (belonging); and personal development and growth opportunities. For some, it offers creativity and self-realization. Intuitively, being unemployed would mean not having or losing such important benefits, and one may thus expect a greater likelihood of detrimental effects on health. On my home front I had witnessed the impact of involuntary unemployment in the first few years of our marriage, when Sudha was unable to work as a physician in Canada.

In the late 1980s and early 1990s, unemployment had risen in Canada and was projected to remain high through the turn of the century. However, the official figure was based on a narrow definition of "the unemployed": those who actively sought work in the preceding four weeks and did not work more than one hour in the previous week. The definition did not include those who chose not to work or weren't available for work for personal reasons or were underemployed. Our findings suggested that, while the unofficial rate of unemployment at that time was 12.4 percent, if we considered the people who came under the more inclusive definition of unemployment, the rate jumped to fifteen percent.

Through a literature search, we found that unemployment is associated with increase in the overall death rates and deaths due to heart diseases as well as suicide. It is associated with increased alcohol consumption and smoking, promotes a sedentary lifestyle and unhealthy dietary habits; with regards to morbidity, it is again associated with increases in the rate of depression and suicidal tendencies, and domestic violence. It also associated with increases admission rates to mental and general hospitals and visits to physicians' offices. We were able to quantify these associated increases and conclude that unemployment is associated with an increase in the number of people dying and suffering from various mental and physical ailments.

Our research thus showed a strong relationship between unemployment and ill health. Canada had a high prevalence of unemployment, and there were high direct health care and societal costs. As of December 1995, 2.5 million unemployed Canadians were in involuntary part-time jobs or were discouraged from seeking work. Unemployment in Canada had reached an epidemic proportion and took a significant toll on Canadians' health.

We further studied the excess utilization of these unemployed workers' health care and estimated the excess costs. Excess utilization occurred in psychiatric and general hospitals, visits to physicians and excess drug use. We developed a mathematical model to estimate the extra cost in health care due to unemployment from available data.

To our surprise this excess cost amounted to 850 million to 1.2 billion dollars in 1994. Armed with this information, and through our committee members, who were also members of the Association of Local Public Health Physicians, I managed to speak at their annual general meeting. AGMs are usually dull and pedantic and do not interest the media, but this time the *Toronto Star* published our findings in a front-page story, titled, "Jobless Sick Bill Hits $1 Billion," and I was deluged with media interviews for radio, television, and print. "The unemployed are more likely than those with jobs to suffer from heart disease, hypertension, suicidal tendencies, depression, insomnia, joint problems, headaches and hay fever, said Dr Chandrakant Shah." (*Toronto Star*, 31 January 1994)

The news made it to the question-answer period in the Canadian Parliament, and we received a request for our report from the health minister of the day. My office was buzzing with calls from the media. What kept me going was the immense gratification I felt on realizing that I had chosen the right strategies for studying the extra burden to the nation's health care costs to draw the attention of the politicians and policymakers and it complemented the work by other activists who had focussed on the personal and social impacts of unemployment. A call from the federal minister's office following a parliamentary question-answer period gave me a lot of satisfaction as our committee's voice had been heard at the highest level where it mattered the most. On the home front my wife Sudha was delighted at the accolades I had received and especially happy to get calls from my friends and their wives expressing their admiration for the work I had done. Finally it felt (I hope) that her sacrifices were not in vain!

On the work front, our committee developed a position paper for the upcoming annual meeting of the Canadian Public Health Association in Halifax, Nova Scotia, and I presented our findings. The Canadian Broadcasting Corporation arranged twelve radio interviews in a single sitting, airing across Canada from east to west. In the end, the hotel telephone operator phoned me and said, "I have never arranged so many interviews in such a short time in my career! You must be an important man." I replied, "I am not an important man, but I had an important message that Canadians needed to hear."

Canada's unemployment rate fell in the early 2000s and again raised its head in 2008 when the world economy went into a major recession, reaching 9–9.5 percent. At this point, I was working as a part-time consultant, advising the Peel Public Health Unit, which covers cities of Brampton, Mississauga and the town of Caledon, on diversity, equity and inclusion.

At the end of it all, I did indeed feel that the major health organizations, the government, and the public had heard my voice and accepted several recommendations.

Homelessness and Health: Heart and Soul

In the winter of 1995, on a freezing early morning I took the subway to work when I noticed a barely dressed man sitting on the train. There was no one sitting in the seat next to him, even though the train was full. I realized that other passengers were shunning him for his appearance. I reasoned in my mind that he was sitting in the train to keep himself warm. I also remembered my situation once, in 1970, when I was returning from India with my wife and one year old son. As London airport was completely fogged, many flights including ours were diverted to Manchester. With the influx of thousands of unannounced passengers like us, the airport ran out of food and benches to sit. We spread a newspaper on the floor and sat or slept on it and were fed by the Salvation Army with soup and buns for which we had to line up. Now on the subway in Toronto I decided to sit next to the barely dressed man, reasoning that he was just another human being whose situation I did not know but surely was dire. While we did not converse, we exchanged glances through the corners of our eyes, acknowledging each other's presence. While leaving the subway car, I asked him whether he was hungry and would accept some of the food I was carrying. He indicated yes by nodding his head. I also noticed the happiness on his face. As I am from India, I had seen abject poverty and homelessness. However, at that time, I may have accepted poverty and homelessness as just a part of life. Now as a Canadian of over forty years, I had changed and was able to see what had been invisible in the past. Hence, this was the first time I became aware of the state of a homeless individual.

A few days later I saw a mother in her twenties with an approximately nine-month-old child sitting at the subway entrance. She was homeless. How could a country like Canada, one with so much wealth, be unable to provide aid for its underprivileged citizens?

Following these two incidents, I began to reflect deeply on home-lessness in Canadian society. These two incidents also happened to coincide with an increase in begging in Toronto due to the 1995 economic downturn and a large public debate about the increasing number of "squeegee kids" in the city.

Since my area of expertise was public health, I decided to analyze the effects of homelessness on health. I was still a member of the Population Health Committee of the Ontario Medical Association. I brought the plight of the homeless to my committee's attention and expressed the urgent need to advocate for their well-being. We looked for any existing literature on homelessness and health. As our investigations progressed, I grew certain that the issue needed more human connection or what I like to call a "heart and soul" to connect with the plight of the homeless—beyond statistics and prognostications.

To consider homelessness is to perceive a range of living arrange-ments and various populations in special circumstances. In 1987, the United Nations, designating the International Year of Shelter for the Homeless, established a distinction between absolute home-lessness, people living on the street and victims of disaster with no homes at all, and relative homelessness, people housed in dwellings that fail to meet basic standards.

The UN went on to identify five such basic standards. Thus, a dwelling must:
1. Adequately protect occupants from the elements.
2. Be provided with safe water and sanitation.
3. Provide for secure tenure and personal safety.
4. Lie within easy reach of employment, education and health care.
5. Be affordable.

Persons living in absolute homelessness are those with no fixed address, including people living on the streets, those using shelters, and, in the case of young children, those provided with shelter in conditions bearing little resemblance to a home, often referred to as welfare motels. By contrast, persons living in relative homelessness are generally housed in a dwelling, but one that is sufficiently derelict as to fall short of the UN's five standards.

Closer to home, the federal Library of Parliament's 1994 paper on homelessness describes three categories: chronic, periodic, and temporary homelessness. Persons facing chronic homelessness are estimated to make up to 20–40 percent of those using emergency shelters or hostels and typically are socially marginalized people, often engaging in substance abuse or exhibiting psychiatric conditions. By contrast, persons facing periodic homelessness generally leave home due to a crisis such as domestic violence or abuse. Still, they may return to such homes after periods in shelters or on the streets. The last group, persons facing temporary homelessness, comprises those who lose their shelter because of fire or flood, hospitalization or unemployment, leading to eviction or foreclosure.

I decided that the best way to understand and develop an emotional connection with and empathy for the homeless would only happen by interacting with the homeless directly, hearing their stories, their trials and tribulations. I strongly believed that effectiveness of advocacy is more credible when one can narrate one's stories from his or her firsthand experience rather than cite statistics. To take this forward, I decided to work in a food bank as many of their clients are homeless. I was acquainted with Gerard Kennedy, manager of the largest food bank in Toronto (many years later, he was a contestant for the leadership of the Liberal Party of Canada). I enquired about the possibility of working as a volunteer in a food bank. He arranged for me to work at one of the largest food banks, giving me a four-hour shift every Saturday morning. As I owned a Mercedes at the time, I was uncomfortable driving it to the food bank. Quite honestly, the car made me feel a bit guilty. Hoping not to draw attention to my status, I always parked my car two blocks away from the food bank and walked the rest of the way. I also dressed as inconspicuously as possible, donning a pair of jeans, which I hardly ever wear outside my home, and a casual shirt.

I asked Gerard to assign me work in the hamper room, where individuals requesting food came, enabling me to interact with them and learn about their situations. On the day of my arrival in the hamper room, I introduced myself as a volunteer to the person in charge, a white man in his fifties. He did not know my background, and I did not see any need to provide it. In his eyes, I was a short, dark, South Asian person, dressed in jeans and a T-shirt. He took one look at me and probably thought he could not trust me to carry out the important duties in the hamper room. Instead, he assigned me a different job, asking me to empty large drums of skim milk into smaller one-pound bags. That morning, I packed more than 200 bags of one-pound skim milk. I was kept in the back room for a few more Saturdays doing mundane work. One Saturday, the volunteer who usually worked in the hamper room did not show up, prompting the supervisor to put me there. I was somewhat excited about this responsibility, which meant that I would be interacting with the very individuals I wanted to.

A couple of weeks into my new role at the food bank, I had a moving experience. A man came in that morning asking for pears. Unfortunately, the food bank did not have fresh fruit, as they distributed only non-perishable food items. Curious about his demand's specificity and his somewhat desperate demeanor, I asked him why he wanted pears so badly. "It's my six-years-old's birthday, and I promised her fresh fruit," he told me. No matter how poor or rich one may be, a parent's love for a child transcends every limitation. I felt overwhelmed by the father's desperate attempt to please his daughter and my powerlessness in helping him do so that day. That memory is still vividly etched in my mind. During my time at the food bank, a story was published about my work on unemployment and health in *Toronto Star*. Gerard came down during my shift to congratulate me. The head of the hamper room was confused by this exchange and promptly asked me who I was.

After three months at the food bank, I felt that it was time for me to move to a setting where I could witness homeless individuals' health issues. I read an article in a newspaper about a medical clinic in a men's homeless shelter looking for a physician to help. The clinic was in a downtown shelter that was only open overnight for homeless men. The shelter could house 400 men, and the current physician, the late Dr Robert Frankford, a past member of the Ontario provincial parliament, could not handle the entire workload by himself. He knew of me as a professor, so I felt comfortable calling him personally to offer my services one day a week. Initially, he was a bit reluctant as I was a university professor, and the fact that I would be working under him made him somewhat uncomfortable. I told him that I had no ego and would be content to work under his leadership; I was a novice in his field and could learn a lot from him. He agreed to take me on. For three months, I worked at the shelter, helping men with their various physical, emotional, and social ailments. One winter morning, a man came to the clinic who had been wandering the streets barefoot the previous night and had severe frostbite on his feet. He had completely lost the thick skin of the soles, exposing the muscles and bones of his feet. This was another moving moment for me and perhaps the most illuminating in understanding the health consequences of homelessness.

I also volunteered for the street patrol program run by the Anishnawbe Health Toronto clinic, catering to mainly Aboriginal homeless people. The street patrol would go out every night in a van visiting the areas where Toronto's homeless population were known to hang out—under bridges, in abandoned warehouses, and in public parks. We distributed sandwiches, soup, blankets, shoes, and socks, and I also provided essential primary medical care out of the van.

During my attempts to understand the plight of the homeless, I came across a woman who had run away from domestic abuse. She came into my clinic demanding to see the doctor and no one else. The receptionist at the desk told her she had to register first as she had never been to our clinic, and then would be seen by the intake nurse, who would decide if she needed to see a doctor. The woman raised her voice and yelled, demanding to see the doctor. I heard this commotion from my office. I came out, saw a distraught tall and stocky woman, and asked the receptionist not to fuss about registration and invited her to come with me to my office. She stood in front of my chair, opened the top two buttons of her blouse and asked me to look at her chest. I noticed a perfect circular second-degree burn, about five centimetres in diameter just above her breast. I asked her, "How did this happen?" She replied that she had spilled scalding coffee. Not believing her explanation, I asked again what had happened. Upset by my insistence, she exclaimed, "I told you it was hot coffee!" Then I told her, "I am your doctor, and it is okay to tell me the truth." Suddenly she lost her balance and fell. I tried to catch her, but because of her weight and height, I could not manage, and we both fell. We both sat on the ground, and she cried for almost five minutes while I comforted her. She then told me that two days ago, she had had arguments with her partner, and in his anger, he had scorched her with a propane torch. She left home and had been on the street for the past two days and nights. She also revealed that she was hospitalized a year ago in another city for a month with a head injury leading to a coma. She told the hospital staff it was due to a fall, when it was due to a blunt instrument that was used to hit her on her head by her partner. It broke my heart to hear her story and to think of the ever-increasing number of women who end up homeless after escaping domestic violence.

All these experiences helped me gain a true understanding of homeless people beyond their statistical profiles. I returned to the Population Health Committee of the OMA. We began to put together a workshop, which involved NGOs, churches, mental health professionals, outreach workers, the OMA, government representatives, and representatives of the Indigenous health and social service centres. We decided not to hold this workshop in a hotel or convention facility or the posh meeting room at the OMA headquarters or the conference room at the university. We held the one-day workshop at Seaton House, a shelter for homeless men. As one of our committee members was suffering from a terminal illness, we called it Dr Martin Bass's Day to honour his legacy and invited him and his family. We had almost 100 people attending, and we discussed issues affecting different groups of homeless individuals and strategies to ameliorate them, including the type of advocacy actions needed.

Dr Brian Hodges, resident physician in Public Health and Preventive Medicine at the Dalla Lana School of Public Health, and I developed a position paper, which was presented at the AGM of the Canadian Public Health Association in 1997. In it we attempted to dispel any false public beliefs, such as that these individuals are homeless by choice or all of them had mental health issues or were addicts, and recommended several actions to be taken.

When I look back, I feel that I tried to raise the issue of homelessness not only as a social or moral issue but also as a health issue. I received support from the OMA, while CPHA adopted our findings and recommendations. It gives me some satisfaction that many health professional educational institutes now include homelessness in their curricula. Many times, we tend to understand these problems only through statistics but never the human emotions that run turbulently behind it. If we change our perspective, we would be able to understand our patients in a better way and only when we understand them can we give them better medical care.

Places of Worship for Minorities

With the liberalization of immigration law in the early 1960s, non-white immigrants from other commonwealth countries started arriving in Canada. As an immigrant from India in 1965, I was aware of the struggle that newcomers faced to adapt to new lifestyles in their adopted country. While they attempted to fit in with the ways of the host society, they continued to maintain as much of their cultural heritage as was practical. This was their right according to the policy of multiculturalism. Religion was a vital cultural heritage. People interact and identify through religious activities and social events; religious gatherings promote social cohesiveness and make adaptation easier. However, one needs infrastructure, described in the sociology literature as social capital. During early settlements in Canada, besides building their homes, the first institutes built by the settlers were churches and schools. Many municipal zoning bylaws required every new development in the settlement to have a church and a primary school within walking distance.

In the 1960s and 1970s, immigrants of South Asian origins began arriving in large numbers, and there was clearly a need for their places of worship, such as temples, mosques, and gurdwaras. Though I was never a regular attendee at Jain temple, I understood the importance of social cohesion, which I strongly believe is promoted by places of worship. I practice Jainism and my religious beliefs have played a significant role in the development of my spiritual values, such as nonviolence, nonmaterialistic living, and acceptance of difference.

Quite a few of the cultural institutions in Canada regularly helped and inspired their members to succeed in life, and I often felt motivated to support them. These sentiments led me to Gujarat Samaj, a group of Hindu Canadians from Gujarat, a state in western India. This group was attempting to build a mandir (temple) in the Greater Toronto Area, that would double up as a place of worship and a community centre. The GTA has historically been a strong immigrant reception region. It has a population of 6.2 million people (2020), of which almost fifty percent are identified as visible minorities representing some 110 countries. The countries of origin of Toronto's immigrant population have significantly changed over time. Over the last sixty years, the number of people from European countries has declined steadily while those from Asian countries increased. Since 2001, the largest number of new immigrants originated from India, followed by China, Pakistan, the Philippines, Sri Lanka, and Iran.

In the 1960s and 70s, many places of worship for recent immigrants, especially those belonging to faiths other than Judeo-Christian, were either hidden in industrial complexes or were far from the city, requiring a great deal of travel. This was largely due to the inability of the newly settled to afford properties in residential areas. In 1976, approximately 10,000 Gujaratis were spread out all over Metro Toronto, mostly in the northeast part of the city. On weekends, many met to pray in the basements of private homes, community centres, or school meeting halls. Even with all the turmoil that came from being newcomers in their adopted country, they cherished celebrating their festivals like Diwali, participating in their native dances like raas-garba or teaching their mother tongue,

Gujarati, to their children. This need for retaining their heritage led to the establishment of the Gujarat Samaj of Toronto in 1970.

In 1977, Gujarat Samaj members began to envision a large, central cultural place. This dream led to the formation of a building committee, whose mandate was to carry out a feasibility study. Within a short period, the committee concluded that the best option was to purchase a piece of land and construct a building to suit their specific needs. The community would have preferred their place of worship nearer to their homes in Toronto but realized that it was not financially feasible. By 1985 the Gujarat Samaj collected about $50,000 for the building fund, and in December that year purchased 9.77 acres of land in the town of Markham for $280,000, away from the City of Toronto.

The community chose Markham because it was situated on a ravine—a preferred site for a Hindu temple is either on a riverbank or ravine. The land was situated in a wealthy white neighbourhood. The Samaj had consulted the City Planning Department about zoning regulations before purchasing the land. The Planning Department assured them that building a place of worship was allowed under existing zoning regulations and asked the community to submit a planning document for approval. After land acquisition, the community enthusiastically endorsed the project, and many individuals stepped forward to volunteer and donate. A sum of $450,000 was pledged.

However, as soon as the wealthy and influential residents of the area, predominantly Christian, found out there would be a Hindu temple in their vicinity, they organized a ratepayers' association, expressing their disapproval to their councillors and mayor. They brought intense pressure upon the City of Markham and even changed the area's zoning bylaws. To appease them, the Council imposed an almost overnight Interim Control By-law, without public consultation, to freeze all new developments, for a one-year period. The Samaj was unaware of this new by-law and continued to proceed with their planning. Before submitting the proposed design blueprints for the building permit, on 29 May 1986 the community leaders met the mayor of Markham, Carole Bell. The mayor informed them that their permit could not be processed due to the new by-law passed two weeks ago.

The Gujarati community mounted a campaign with an appeal to the Markham Planning Department to repeal the zoning by-law. As a member of the community, I had supported the project with my donation, though I was not an active member of any committee. I started taking an active interest in the matter. I began to speak on the community's behalf, aiding them in their extensive preparations for the appeal, giving media interviews, and becoming their de facto spokesperson. Our appeal was rejected in February 1987.

Following this, we decided to present a petition signed by Markham residents to their City Council to repeal the by-law. We went door to door, explaining our situation and appealing to people to sign the petition. Most inhabitants signed our petition, while a few asked us to "go back home and pray to your God in your homeland. This is a Christian country." Of course, this hurt but it did not deter us.

Over the summer, we collected over 10,000 signatures and presented them to City Council. A few councillors were supportive of our cause. During this period, there was a municipal election, and our group become politically active, canvassing for the mayoral candidate who opposed the incumbent. Mayor Carol Bell lost the election. The new mayor appointed a special committee consisting of four councillors and a chair to conduct a public hearing and forward their decision to City Council for approval.

The public hearing took place in a hall at one of the community centres with a seating capacity for approximately 150 persons. We had advertised heavily about this hearing, and so did the local ratepayers' association. As this issue had galvanized our community, almost 300 Gujarat Samaj members showed up; the meeting hall was overcrowded, there was no room even to stand! I was the spokesperson for our group. Before the hearing began, one of us discovered that the ratepayers' association, as a tactic to cancel the hearing, had called and complained to the fire department about a fire hazard. That person came and whispered the news in my ears. I lost not a moment and did what came naturally to me—get into action mode. I reached for the microphone and announced to our group about the fire hazard due to overcrowding and requested them to return to their homes so that the hearing could start. It was a tough request, as many of these community members had put in long hours of work into furthering our appeal and wanted to show their continued support. Eventually, understanding the gravity of the situation, most of them left, leaving behind fifty or so members, and we began to plead our case.

I made an impassioned speech for our need for a place of worship, how the city's planning department had assured us about the then existing zoning by-law, permitting us to build a place of worship, how the city changed the by-law overnight without any public hearing and how that was unjust and discriminatory. We were fortunate to have a priest from the Christian faith speaking on our behalf and appealing to the councillors that "we are all children of God."

The opposition said the temple would generate a huge amount of traffic with worshippers flocking on weekends and holidays, ruining their quiet and tranquil neighbourhood. They also expressed concerns about the possibility of their property losing value on account of the temple's presence. The committee members asked several pertinent questions to both sides, and things went smoothly until the committee vote. The Chair usually abstained from the voting, and the four other council members were responsible for making a ruling. However, the votes were evenly split, two apiece, and the Chair was forced to vote to break the tie. There was a great deal of suspense and an eerie silence in the hall. After a few moments of trepidation, the Chair voted in our favour, eliciting exclamations and tears of joy from the remaining Samaj members, as well as myself. In disbelief, we hugged each other and believed that our prayers were finally answered. Till today I cannot forget hugging my elder son and the tears of joy in our committee members. Momentarily, we felt that this decision had cleared obstacles in our path.

The committee's decision was forwarded to the Regional Municipality of York, which now referred the matter to the Town of Markham for reconsideration. However, numerous objections began to come in from residents again stating that the temple would disrupt their way of life. It is interesting that Canada was trumpeting the Hindu communities' existence as integral to the nation's multicultural identity during this time! These dissidents started collecting funds to take the matter to the Ontario Municipal Board. We realized that as newcomers we could not match those deep pockets challenging our case. We accepted the fact that while we had won the battle, we were losing the war!

However, Markham City Council appointed Tony Roman, then the mayor of Markham, to a one-member committee that would resolve the issue. At this time the real-estate market was performing remarkably well. Mayor Roman was a great friend and wellwisher of our community. He proposed that the City of Markham allow our group to rezone the existing site into seven residential estate lots to conform to the neighbourhood's zoning and secure an alternative site for our temple with institutional zoning. The real-estate agent estimated these lots could sell well and get more than $400,000 each, generating total revenue worth $2.8 million; this would enable us to acquire a fully serviced site for our centre and even have some funds left over after the mandir's construction. The local residents were happy that finally they would get rid of these undesirable Hindu neighbours! It appeared to be a win-win for both parties. Unfortunately, before we could put these lots on the market, real-estate rates plunged and all our hopes were dashed.

The rezoning of the existing site and selection of an alternative site took its time and toll. We acquired the present five-acre site on 23 October 1992, for $1,919,000 and our previously owned 9.2 acres of land sold for merely $950,000 instead of the earlier estimate of $2.8 million. We were again the losers. However, we managed. Donations poured in, outdoor religious services were held, and finally on 21 October 1994, at a Diwali celebration and fundraising dinner, the Minister of Citizenship, Elaine Ziemba, presented the group with a cheque for $750,000 on behalf of the Government of Ontario.

The Sanatan Mandir Cultural Centre is the result of twenty years of struggle. Not everyone involved in this passion project had the time, convenience, or financial means to set up something so grand in scale. Despite other commitments and responsibilities, these individuals, with their exemplary dedication and persistence, helped create a centre that became a landmark for the Gujarati Hindu community in Canada that will be cherished by many generations to come.

14

Transforming Public Health Education

Teaching Public Health

One of my responsibilities in the Department of Preventive Medicine at the University of Toronto was to teach medical students about public health in Canada. The subject of public health occupied one-sixth of the final national licensing examination of the Medical Council of Canada; the other five were medicine, surgery, pediatrics, obstetrics and gynecology, and psychiatry. While reviewing the existing course in public health, I observed that there was no formal coherent curriculum for undergraduate students. Instead, the course consisted of a series of lecture notes compiled over the years. I was, of course, not in charge of the undergraduate program but just one of many who taught the relevant material. I was not even a course director for any of the six cognate disciplines taught under the rubric of public health, viz. epidemiology, biostatistics, health care systems, behavioural sciences, occupational and environmental health, and preventive medicine.

Initially the six cognate disciplines of public health were taught during the first two years of the medical undergraduate program in different modules. As is the case with any undergraduate or postgraduate program, there will always be that one subject that would seem like your nemesis! The course in public health was one of those! Most of the material was dull and not taught by the clinicians but by nonclinical faculties such as biostatisticians, epidemiologists, behaviour scientists, and health administrators, and students failed to understand the relevance of a subject to their future careers as clinical practitioners. It's like how some of my friends who always had a bent of mind for the arts felt for a subject like trigonometry in school! Therefore, most students despised the course. The only salvation for public health teachings was that one-sixth of the students' licensing exam was based on the subject material taught in this course.

I found this disheartening. I decided to find out how it was in other medical schools. I carried out an "environment scan" by sending a questionnaire asking several pointed questions to the departments in the other fifteen medical schools in Canada. It appeared that they had similar issues, such as lack of overall curricula objectives, teaching done by assorted nonclinical faculties, and students' scepticism regarding the relevance of the material taught.

I then presented these results at the national meeting of Teachers of Social and Preventive Medicine, the group responsible for teaching public health at all medical schools. I proposed a national workshop to define our course objectives and desired competencies in our field. This proposal was welcomed. During this period, public health as a discipline was going through a crisis of identity and was seeking to find its relevance and place within the health care system. In some circles, it was now called Community Health/Medicine.

Following this enthusiastic approval, I applied to Health Canada and the Hospital for Sick Children Foundation, requesting their support for such a workshop. I received modest financial grant from the Hospital for Sick Children Foundation. In 1976 then, I invited representatives from all medical school departments of social and preventive medicines and a few clinicians in the country to a workshop designed to establish a public health curriculum which would be relevant to clinical practice. The final report of the workshop with recommendations was published in English and French (official languages of Canada) in the *Canadian Journal of Public Health* in 1980. But having a report is one thing, for it to be implemented would need more work. This was achieved through another national workshop and a taskforce and finally the Medical Council of Canada adopted the recommendations as a basis for the medical licensing exam. It was a great accomplishment for public health and public health teachers to be equal partners with the other five clinical disciplines. This document became the foundation for the development of course curricula across all medical schools.

Transforming Public Health into a Profession

Public health is organized differently in the different Canadian provinces. However, common to them all is the fact that they all have Medical Officers of Health at the local and provincial levels responsible for their community. The officer of health is a physician who, before 1976, did not require to be trained in public health or had a one-year diploma in public health from the School of Hygiene at the University of Toronto or similar programs in the US or UK.

The Royal College of Physicians and Surgeons of Canada (RCPSC) is the national examining and certifying body for medical specialists. It establishes standards for specialty medical education and accredits the residency programs and learning activities at all of Canada's seventeen medical schools. Since 1947, public health as a specialty had been dormant, except in British Columbia, where a relatively small number of physicians had acquired the specialist certificate in public health. However, there were still no formalized four-year training programs due to a lack of demand for public health departments.

In 1974, under the leadership of the late Dr Donald Anderson from the University of British Columbia, a group of professionals in public health realized that public health as a specialty needed a revival. The Royal College of Physicians and Surgeons of Canada set up a task force which recommended that a specialty of public health and preventive medicine be created and named "Community Medicine." They also mandated a five-year training program with the requirement that the trainee spend two years in a clinical discipline training program, do a year of course work in the basic disciplines of public health, and spend the remaining time in the field. In recent years, the specialty of community medicine has been renamed and is now known as public health and preventive medicine.

Under the Constitutional Act of Canada (1982), the provinces are primarily responsible for their population's health. This then implies that the provinces decide the needs for their human resources; they allocate the number of trainees needed in different specialities and pay their salaries, since these individuals, while in training, provide clinical services in hospitals.

I was appointed the inaugural director of the residency training program in Public Health and Preventive Medicine at the University of Toronto in 1976 even though I was only certified by the Royal College in pediatrics; I did not have any trainees nor the required funding to hire any if they applied or any administrative support; further, there was also no defined curriculum. In those days, there was no statutory requirement for public health units to hire medical officers of health with specialist certificates; there was no demand for a four-year trained specialist in public health.

We were determined that public health as a specialty occupy a status similar to internal medicine, surgery, radiology, etc. With the help of the chair of the department of health administration Dr Eugene Vayda, we were able to secure funding from the Ontario Ministry of Health for sixteen residents over a five-year period. I also capitalized on the opportunities to secure alternative funding sources for residents, sponsored by the Canadian Cancer Society, the Canadian Armed Forces, and the Government of Saudi Arabia. Realizing that some of the smaller universities might not be able to develop their own five-year programs, I started a relationship with the University of Saskatchewan, Dalhousie University, and Memorial University and invited them to be affiliated institutions with our program, where we trained their chosen residents for the first two years, after which they returned to their provinces for field training. While they were in their field training, I was required to visit them every six months to assure quality control. Within the first ten years, we developed a cadre of twenty-six residents, bringing training funds of over one million dollars—the largest training program in public health in North America at that time.

Similar to the undergraduate curriculum in public health, there was a need for standardized competencies for the practice of a public health specialist. I secured the necessary fund and called for a national workshop on the development of objectives for Residency Training in Community Medicine; this was held in 1988–89. A detailed document was produced, adopted in 1994 by the Specialty Committee in Community Medicine, The Royal College of Physicians and Surgeons of Canada (RCPSC).

I also made sure that the national examination conducted by the RCPSC for specialist status was the same in English and French. During the late 1980s and early 1990s there were numerous federal and provincial task forces and commissions related to health care delivery, but astonishingly there was a singular absence of public health specialists at the decision tables. This was remedied.

In our program, residents came from different disciplines, and they all contributed greatly with their observations and suggestions. As the manager, I made decisions to prioritize the program's integrity over the preference of the residents. In 1984, three residents expressed their unhappiness at my ruling on moonlighting. Also, as it happened, out of five residents appearing for the Royal College final exam, only one passed. This made the residents more discontented, and they questioned my suitability as a program director. Without lodging any formal complaint with the associate dean or me, this group of three sought help from the Association of Local Public Health Agencies (ALPHA), listing a litany of complaints against the program and me. They requested ALPHA to write a letter to the Ontario minister of health to impeach me, accusing me of program mismanagement, including misuse of their trust funds. Until then, the word "impeachment" had never entered my vocabulary! As I had no signing authority on the funds, their claim had no validity. I confronted ALPHA with the facts and legal threats of defamation if they pursued writing a letter to the minister, and they dropped the issue. I must say that all my colleagues, including my dean, were extremely supportive. Following this, some ALPHA members and my associate dean asked me if this episode was motivated by racism on the part of the three white residents and a few of the ALPHA board members. As I was still quite oblivious to unconscious bias, I replied, "I hope not."

In 1988, I retired from the program after serving for twelve exciting years. Now almost fifty percent of all the medical officers of health in Canada were trained fully or partially at the University of Toronto. Our graduates had a great impact on public and population health in Canada and even abroad. Many of them went on to head major universities and medical organizations, and some received international acclaim. Dr David Butler Jones was the inaugural Chief Medical Officer of Health, Public Health Agency of Canada; Dr Vivek Goel was the inaugural Director of Ontario Public Health and now is president of the University of Waterloo; Dr Kue Young became the Dean, School of Public Health, the University of Alberta; Doctors Colin D'Cunha, Sheela Basrur, Richard Schabas, and David Williams became Ontario's Chief Medical Officers of Health; Dr Steven Narod is internationally known for his research on breast cancer. To be a medical officer of health at the local, regional, or provincial level, one now requires to be a trained and certified public health specialist—a great triumph for the specialty of public health.

In appreciation of my contribution, on my retirement from the residency program, my division established an endowment for the CP Shah Residency Award to be given annually given to a resident who carries out the best field project in public health. I get invited to present the award every year. I feel proud to see the specialty not only maturing but also flourishing. The SARS epidemic and the COVID-19 pandemic have highlighted the role of public health specialists and names like Sheela Basrur, Bonnie Henry, David Williams, and Howard Njoo—our former trainees—have become household names!

15

A Canadian Textbook on Public Health

During my involvement in public health education starting in 1974 there was no comprehensive textbook on the subject in Canada. Coming from a pediatric background, I was aware of textbooks in all clinical, medical, and surgical specialties. Many of these textbooks were dubbed as "a Bible" to be studied and kept forever. As the description and management of diseases or procedures are universal for clinical subjects, it did not matter whether authors published the books in the US, the UK or elsewhere. However, it did matter when it pertained to public health in Canada. There are country-specific legislations dealing with infectious diseases and environmental and occupational regulations; evolution, organization, and financing of health care delivery. There are problems specific to a culture and country. I began to contact other people in Canadian universities in the hopes of discovering a textbook that would encompass the public health topics my courses included, but to no avail. As it happened, I did come across an American textbook edited by a Canadian, the late Dr John Last. This lack of comprehensive material within a single source troubled me deeply.

I decided that a textbook had to be written as soon as possible. I contacted the Canadian Association of Teachers of Social and Preventative Medicine in the hopes of them commissioning a multi-authored textbook. Their executives approved the idea, but it never materialized. Finally, out of desperation, in 1982, I solicited my colleague the late Dr Peter Morgan to be the co-editor. For almost a year, he did not produce a single chapter, and I realized that Peter's skills were primarily in editing and not necessarily in writing. Finally, I decided I could no longer wait. Peter also left the department and became one of the finest editors for the *Canadian Medical Association Journal*. Meanwhile I also asked my department to commission such a book in which different chapters could be written by experts in different disciplines of public health. This was agreed, but somehow the book did not materialize.

Due to other commitments, it took me about four years to complete a draft, at which point I submitted the outline and sample chapters to publishers. The first publisher took three months to respond before rejecting it; the second one took nine months, the reason being that there was no market for such a book. This was sheer short-sightedness and ignorance. A third publisher also rejected it for the same reason. At this point, in 1984, I lost all hope of ever publishing it, and the draft manuscript was filed in my cabinet, gathering dust.

In 1986, while attending a meeting related to public health in Toronto, I struck up a conversation with my colleague Susan Ever, who informed me that she was teaching public health in Canada to life science students at the University of Waterloo. She lamented the fact that she too had no real textbook. I mentioned that I had the draft of one, which greatly delighted her. I ended up inviting her back to my office that very day to show her my manuscript. After skimming through the manuscript for a few minutes, she told me that it was exactly what she was looking for and asked me if she could photocopy fifty copies for her class. I told her that I would be happy to give her the copies but only after I had made some much-needed revisions to outdated facts and figures.

I spent that entire summer working on the textbook, adding new content. I took the help of my elder son, Sunil, who had just turned eighteen and had mastered the skill of typing. Sunil also became my de facto editor correcting my grammatical errors and poor sentence structure as we revised the textbook. After we had gone through the entire book, we started printing it. I titled the book *The Canadian Health and Health Care System*. I initially made a hundred copies, of which I shipped fifty to Dr Ever as promised, and within a few months, the remaining books were gone as people began to discover it. We went back and made even more copies, the demand greatly outstripping our system of supply. I had always been convinced that there was a need for such a book in health sciences courses across Canada and, finally, my dream became a reality.

Sunil, by using the PageMaker publishing program, was able to reduce the book's size from 375 pages to 150 pages, cutting the time and cost of printing. The second edition was published in 1987. But after the next two years I noticed that it was not gaining as much traction as I had expected within medical schools, which was a rather large market. I realized that the book needed a couple of more chapters to be as comprehensive as needed. To signify this change, I changed the title to *Public Health and Preventive Medicine in Canada*. This time I hired a professional editor, indexer, and proofreader. News of this new book slowly started to spread, and, before long, I had to go to the University of Toronto's printing press to keep pace with the demand. In 1990, the second edition came out with new data, shortly followed by the third edition in 1994, which was translated into French in 1995 by a colleague of mine, the late Dr Fernand Turcotte of Laval University in Québec, making my textbook one of the few bilingual textbooks in Canada

(*Medicine preventive et santé publique au Canada* by Shah C P, with Shah Sunil and Shah Rajiv, Adaptation Francaise sous la direction de Fernand Turcotte, Les Presses de Université Laval, Saint-Foy, 1995; pp. 1–400.) This edition added a special chapter that focused on the health care system in Québec.

As the author, editor, and publisher of the book, I had no outlet for distribution. My house became a storage place for boxes of books, and my wife, Sudha, became distributor and manager of our little business. None of us knew much about business—I did not know what an invoice was or what consignment meant, and we had to start learning about dispatcher and parceling services slowly.

The book became a widely used medical textbook and was found on several prominent recommended book lists for health sciences courses in Canada. It became a required text for medical undergraduates at reputed universities such as the University of British Columbia, McGill University, and many others and all twelve technical colleges that taught Health Record Administration across Canada. The Medical Council of Canada recommended it for their licensing examination and it was also recommended for graduate courses in Community Health across Canada. Over 30,000 copies of this book across Canada have been used to date. A fourth edition was published in 1998 but was not translated into French. The fifth edition came out in 2003.

While publishing the fifth edition, I met a book salesperson from Elsevier Canada, a publishing company that owns the rights to fifty-five percent of the entire medical and health-related textbooks sold in Canada and worldwide. They were quite aware of my book and had initially offered to distribute it, but I didn't like their terms and declined the offer. They came back with a new offer, asking to buy all the rights to the book. I was sixty-seven at the time, and I knew that a book like this needed revision every five years. I wasn't sure if I wanted to begin the long revision process again when I was seventy-two years old, so I decided to listen to their offer. Our talks broke down, but eventually we could meet halfway, and I sold the book rights to them.

It was easy to identify me if you had read the book. One day, while taking the subway to downtown Toronto, a young man came up to me and promptly blurted out, "You're Dr Shah!" He explained that he was a medical student in my university, and just the previous night he had been poring over my book for his final exam that day. He then asked me to sign his book.

This kind of recognition became more frequent and embarrassing. In December 2019, while crossing a street in downtown Toronto, I fell and was taken to the emergency room at St Michael's Hospital. A physician came to my room and when I introduced myself, his expression changed from blank to amazement. He asked me if I was the same Dr Shah of the public health book. I nodded. He said he had graduated two decades ago and had thrown away all his under-graduate books except this one. He still refers to it from time to time, and it was well-spent money. This was terribly moving.

The fifth edition has so far sold 12,500 copies and has been in the top ten or top twenty in various bestselling categories on Amazon.

The Sixth Edition

Sales had started to decline as the contents of the book became outdated. Elsevier had promised to continue re-publishing the book every few years to update its contents. A few years down the road, I reminded them of their promise. But a restructuring of management had occurred, and I almost gave up hopes of a revision. It was hard on me. In 2017, I wrote to their content strategist (acquisitions editor) Roberta Spinosa-Millman, stating that a long time had elapsed since the fifth edition. I also wrote a comment from a student on the internet: "It is essential to obtain a copy of *Public Health and Preventive Medicine in Canada*, by Chandrakant P Shah. It is a blue paperback available on Amazon and in most Canadian medical libraries. This is the de facto Bible for the community health questions on the MCCQE." I wrote to her that if it were the Bible, it was the Old Testament now, and we needed the New Testament. Somehow it got the ball rolling. They offered me authorship, but at eighty-one I was in no mood to do extensive revisions. However, I accepted the role of a consultant to guide the new authors and retain the book's soul. We were fortunate to find two fine authors, Dr Bonnie Fournier, nursing professor at Thompson River University in Kamloops, and Dr Fareen Karachiwalla, associate medical officer of York Region in Ontario. Elsevier decided to honor my legacy by calling the sixth edition *Shah's Public Health and Preventive Health Care in Canada*.

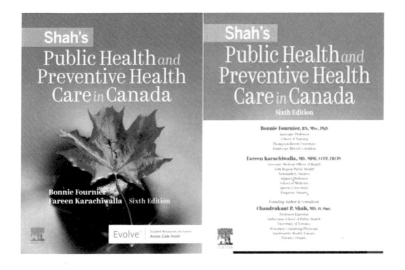

16

Mentorships

As a professor, one influences and shapes many young minds, which one is not aware of until many years later. I was fortunate that many of my students became public health leaders, great researchers, teachers, and social activists. When I see them on television, hear them on the radio, read about them in the newspapers, read their books and journal articles, I am consumed by a great sense of pride. I also feel a sense of gratitude when they mention that I was their mentor or choose to work with the Indigenous community as I had inspired them through my teaching.

One student who became prominent, and indeed a household name in Toronto and Canada, was the late Dr Sheela Basrur. She was the Medical Officer of Health in Toronto during the SARS crisis in 2003, a most calming and reassuring voice then. I first met her in August 1983. She had just returned from India and Nepal, where she had gone to do volunteer work after graduating from medical school as a general practitioner. During her work there, she deduced that the best solution to ameliorate health problems was to prevent disease and promote health and well-being in society. She realized also that she needed training in public health. I was the program director for training physicians in public health, and our new students started on the first of July. Physicians had to apply almost nine months ahead of time to be accepted into the program, and here was this young lady who wanted to start training right now. My routine answer would have been to tell her to apply for the following year, but I felt there was something different about this petite woman (Ontario Premier McGuinty later nicknamed her Mighty Mouse). I saw that she was full of conviction—she wanted to make a difference to help human suffering. So I broke all university rules and admitted her to my program as a resident even though she was five weeks late. I did not have even the salary to pay her. I never regretted my decision, on the contrary, I have patted myself on the back for taking this idealistic woman who made a difference in Ontario and Canada.

As with my other students, I got to know her well, was introduced to her parents, and got invited to her wedding. I became her mentor. Once she entered the job market, she climbed heights quickly and in 1999 was appointed the first Medical Officer of Health for the amalgamated City of Toronto, the largest health unit in the country. Following the SARS epidemic, she was appointed Chief Medical Officer of Health of Ontario. To celebrate her appointment, she had a small dinner party consisting of her parents, one other close family couple, and my wife and I. In her position, she was invited to speak frequently at meetings, conferences, workshops, etc, and if I happened to be in the audience, she would always acknowledge me as her mentor. For a teacher, there is no greater satisfaction than being acknowledged by his or her student!

Unfortunately, during the midst of her flourishing career, she developed cancer. She kept in close contact with many, including me. I was surprised to receive a call from her just three weeks before her death in 2008. The University of Toronto had chosen her to receive an honorary degree, and she wanted me to accept the degree on her behalf. I hesitated and suggested she ask her parents (father a radiation oncologist and mother a professor), her sister, or her daughter (who was sixteen)—and without any hesitation, she mentioned that her wish was that I, as her mentor, should be the one. I was dumbfounded. A week before her death I was accepting on her behalf her degree and delivering a convocation speech. I had to think hard for the speech, always keeping in mind what Sheela would have said had she been there. I decided that the speech's theme should portray what she stood for: Conviction, Commitment, Courage, Connectivity, and Communication.

The Aboriginal Health Centre where I was working had hired a new nurse practitioner in 2002. As part of her orientation, she saw me and immediately hugged and thanked me. She was an immigrant Black woman from the West Indies. I was awestruck by her embrace and asked her what I had done to deserve it. She told me that I had lectured her undergraduate nursing class on Indigenous health; she had been inspired and decided to work in the remote, isolated nursing station in the Sioux Lookout Zone First Nations Community called Sachigo Lake. After working for a few years, she felt she needed more education to serve them better and had enrolled in the Nurse Practitioners Program, which she had just finished. Before she returned to the north, she wanted to work with me and learn more.

In 2005 I received a call from a family physician, Dr D Jakubovicz, of St Michael's Hospital. She identified herself as a program director of a newly created Indigenous Health Fellowship program for family physicians who desired to have a one-year additional training in Indigenous health before working in an Indigenous community. She wanted to place one of her trainees at the Anishnawbe Health Centre where I was working for field experience and asked me whether I would be agreeable to supervise that trainee for three to six months. I had not heard of such a program, so I asked her about its genesis. She told me that a few years back, during her undergraduate course in medical school, I had lectured her class, and this had sparked her interest in Indigenous health, and since then she has been actively promoting it.

My final example is about a philanthropist, Dr Michael Dan, to whom I was introduced first in 2009. He donated ten million dollars to establish the Waakebiness-Bryce Institute for Indigenous Health at the Dalla Lana School of Public Health (my earlier workplace), University of Toronto. At one of our gatherings, he publicly acknowledged that I had sparked his interest in Indigenous health by my lecture when he was a medical student. When he received his honorary doctorate from the University of Toronto, he requested me to be one of the two esquires in the Chancellor's procession leading him to the convocation hall.

The following is a letter I received on Father's Day in 2017 from the late Dr Linda Panaro, who succumbed to Lou Gehrig's Disease and died in 2018 at fifty-seven. She was my resident in the public health and preventive medicine program in 1984 and an exceptional student, who did her first-year residency in plastic surgery at McGill University and then switched to our public health program. During her training, I used to be approached by some of her professors, wanting to talk to me about their concerns about her. Right away I would interject and ask whether she was knitting in their class. I would say to them that Linda can perform two or more tasks simultaneously, and she was receiving straight As in all her courses. They would leave my office surprised but disgruntled. She was also a brilliant teacher. During her career, she was the director of the Federal Field Epidemiology Program, training many epidemiologists across Canada.

Dear Papaji,

I don't know whether you know the impact that you have made on your students' lives. You have influenced so many people for so many years that maybe you take it all for granted. I hope that you know that my career would literally have not been what it was without your guidance, and likewise, my life would not be what it was without your loving hand and listening ear. I told you once that I only had two mentors in my life before I met you—Leonardo da Vinci (who influenced me to write all my biology notes backwards in high school) and Terry Fox (courage in the face of pain and mortality). Neither of them could meet me the way you did—whenever I needed someone wiser. Thank you for always being there when I needed you, Chan!

In my journey through life, I am surprised at how few people seem to value wisdom or look up from the activities of their ordinary activities to ask what it all means. In the field of the Epi Program, evaluators of our trainees focused on the competencies that they were supposed to acquire even though everyone's experiences/activities may be different, but we sought to evaluate a common set of competencies.

Thank you for being both knowledgeable and wise so that I could see the difference between the two.

There are many others.

In summary, I dreamed of being a pediatrician and became a public health expert which provided an immense opportunity to transform medical undergraduate and postgraduate education in public health in Canada; to develop a unique textbook eventually bearing my name and mentoring outstanding public health leaders.

I could not have asked for anything better.

I had a very fulfilling life as a professor, physician, advocate and family man. Over the years, many people, professionals and lay persons contributed to my success and ideals. I thank them all and hope my memoir helps and inspires you to do what you cherish and be who you want to be.

Shah with his classmates from The B J Medical College, Ahmedabad (1961): Sitting, Somabhai Patel, Standing from L to R: Mukti Chhatpar (Lang), Dilip Shah, Chandrakant Shah, Mehru Kapadia, Hansa Gandhi (Modi).

Shah and his younger brother Yogesh in 1960.

Shah Family: Sitting: Sudha & Chandrakant; Standing from L to R: Anita (grand-daughter); Sunil (son); Neha (granddaughter); and Rajiv (son).

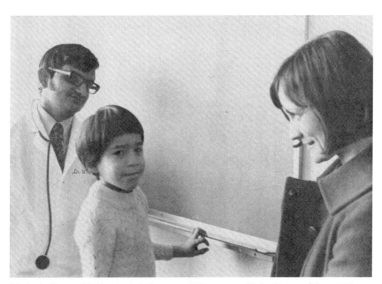

Medical Clinic, Children's Aid Society of Vancouver; Shah, Patient (L) and Foster Mother, 1970.

Presentation of Blanket on Shah's Retirement from the Anishnawbe Health Toronto in 2016. From left to right, Mark McLean (Board Member), Chandrakant Shah, and Joe Hester (Executive Director).

C P Shah beside Cessna float plane, visiting Wapekeka First Nations Community (pop 350) in northern Ontario.

From left to right, Sudha, Phil Fontaine, Chief of Assembly of First Nations, and Chandrakant Shah. Visiting Lectureship on Native Health: Family Violence; September 1992.

Presenting the C P Shah Alumni Award of Excellence to late Dr Sheela Basrur, 2007.

Sudha and Chandrakant Shah on a visit to Chichen Itza Maya Pyramid in Mexico, 2014

Chandrakant and Sudha Shah in their backyard, 2021, while receiving Doctor of Science, honoris causa.

Elder Lillian McGregor on presentation of Eagle Feather to Dr C P Shah, 1999.

Afterword

Dr Shah was the program director when I started as a Community Medicine Resident at the University of Toronto in 1986. At that time he was already an established professor in the Department of Preventive Medicine and Biostatistics. He soon became an important mentor and guide for me, not only during my training, but throughout my career.

This memoir is a testament to the difficult path he has followed through his life and career and his perseverance in the face of innumerable adversities that confronted him and his family. In all the years I have known him he rarely spoke of these difficulties. Rather, he always focused his attention on those around him, particularly those who needed help and support.

It was particularly moving for me to read in these pages about his relationship with his wife and children, and the sacrifices they made as a family while he focused on his career and his causes. There was no shortage of causes, and they continue to this day. He never shied away from issues of injustice and inequity. Over many years, he consistently devoted significant time, energy and personal resources to them despite the toll on the home front.

As I moved through successively more senior administrative roles in different organizations, he was always there to support me—and to remind me of what I could do to advance equity, diversity, and inclusion in those organizations—often in ways that were not always comfortable! But that was the way in which he ensured action happened.

He introduced me and other trainees to the history of colonization of this land and the adverse impact it had on Indigenous peoples, long before there was more mainstream discussion of these topics. His advice and guidance has been invaluable as I and our entire nation have learned about the significance of Truth and Reconciliation, something Dr Shah was committed to long before the formal Commission.

I thank him, and his family, for his tremendous contributions—what he has accomplished has truly changed our world.

Vivek Goel, CM
President and Vice-Chancellor
University of Waterloo

Acknowledgements

At times, our own light goes out and is rekindled by a
spark from another person. Each of us has cause to think
with deep gratitude of those who have lighted the flame
within us.

ALBERT SCHWEITZER

It is believed in many philosophies that when you attach a good
cause to your work, help will flow in miraculously. I was very fortunate to receive tremendous support from my colleagues, friends,
family members, Indigenous people, foundations, civil servants,
politicians, professional organizations, voluntary organizations, the
media and the general public. Without their engagement I would
have accomplished very little, and I would not have stories to tell.

I had many students who went on to occupy seats of responsibility in various organizations. I was able to call upon them to lend me
appropriate organizational support. When I was struggling with the
lack of visible minority representation at the University of Toronto,
I received unsolicited help from faculty members and students from
my department and also from the faculties of arts and science, law,
and education. Community groups brought two busloads of members to the downtown campus of the University of Toronto and

filled up the convocation hall at the public meeting we held to show their support.

I wish to thank all Indigenous and non-Indigenous committee members for guiding me in developing themes and suggesting appropriate speakers. A special note of thanks to the Indigenous speakers across Canada for spending their valuable time teaching and engaging their audiences and the late Phil Jackson and Miriam Johnston for their unwavering support for the program. I'd also like to thank my department chairs, Dr Mary Jane Ashley and Dr Harvey Skinner, for their encouragement and financial support, and also to the PSI Foundations, the Hospital for Sick Children Foundations, and the Governments of Canada and the Province of Ontario. I thank Dr Robert Morgan for transforming me into a public health physician from a pediatrician, and the late Dr Harry Bain for introducing me to Indigenous people.

My heartfelt appreciation to Doctors Rajbir Klair, Allison Reeves, and Harvey Manning for their invaluable help in carrying out research, and Mr Alexander Gomes for help in the preparation of the early manuscript. Special thanks to the visionary Joe Hester for his invitation to work at AHT. His guidance and unwavering support and faith enabled me in my work at Anishnawbe Health Toronto; without it I would not have been able to carry out what I did in my so-called postretirement years.

During my work on the Visiting Lectureship on Native Health, students and faculties from the Universities of Toronto, Ryerson (now Toronto Metropolitan University), and York were at the forefront, promoting the events; many of them did not even know who I was, but they believed in the cause.

I would like to express my sincere gratitude to the churches, other faith communities, foundations, media, and service clubs like Lions and Rotary—each of these organizations did their best to help me raise funds for the new Indigenous health centre.

In 2019, I was petitioning Canadian Blood Services to have inclusion and diversity on its board and upper management. Again, I was astounded by the help I received from my younger brother Yogesh, and Devika, Koki, and Dhaval in collecting more than one thousand signatures. My wife Sudha, sons Sunil and Rajiv, and granddaughters Anita and Neha supported my work, never complained about my absence from home on weekends or for any extended travel. Without their unconditional support, I would not be who I am today.

Thanks to Rashmi Menon for early edits; and Dr Anand Pandya, Darlene Varaleau, Ishan Aditya, Paresh Shah, Dr Suzanne Stewart, and Mark Blair for reading the manuscript and providing useful suggestions for the revision. Finally, and most importantly, I would like to thank my publisher Nurjehan Aziz and my editor MG Vassanji from Mawenzi House, Toronto, for their valuable suggestions and enormous editing efforts in transforming my clumsy scientific writing to a personalized humanistic account of my work.

Chandrakant P Shah, Professor Emeritus at the Dalla Lana School of Public Health, University of Toronto, is a retired physician, public-health practitioner, and advocate for improving the health and well-being of marginalized groups in Canada. He was a professor in the Department of Public Health Sciences, the University of Toronto from 1972–2001. After he retired from the University, he worked at the Anishnawbe Health Centre Toronto from 2001–2016, where he provided primary health care to Indigenous people in Toronto; he also conducted research on urban Indigenous health issues. His research and advocacy work on employment equity had a profound impact on Canadian universities' hiring policies.

He initiated many changes in Canadian society, including amendments to the citizenship examination to include substantial content on Indigenous history. For many years he was actively involved with the development of undergraduate and postgraduate medical education in public health. His important work in developing teaching objectives in medical schools has been vital to their curricula. His textbook, *Shah's Public Health and Preventive Health Care in Canada*, was the first of its kind and is a unique resource widely used in universities.

The University of Toronto has established in his honour the CP

Shah Alumni Award of Excellence in Public Health, the Queen
Elizabeth II/CP Shah Graduate Scholarships in Science, and the C P
Shah Award to a resident in Public Health and Preventive Medicine
for the best research in fieldwork.

Awards

1. University of Toronto: Honorary Degree of Doctor of Science,
   honoris causa, 2021.
2. Gujarat Public Affairs Council of Canada: Gujarat Gaurav Award
   (Pride of Gujarat), 2017.
3. Ontario Ministry of Health and Long Term: Minister's Medal
   Honouring Excellence in Health Quality and Safety, Individual
   Champion 2014.
4. Association of Ontario Health Centres, 2014 Health Equity
   Award for Indigenous Cultural Safety Awareness Initiative.
5. The Canadian Race Relation Foundation, Award of Excellence:
   Honourable Mention in Best Practice Award, 2012.
6. Queen Elizabeth II Silver Jubilee Medal, 2012.
7. 2010 J S Woodsworth Award, for outstanding Commitment
   and Excellence in the Fight for the Elimination of Racial
   Discrimination by the Ontario New Democratic Party.
8. Outstanding Physicians of Ontario in 2007 by the Council of the
   College of Physicians and Surgeons of Ontario.
9. CAPIH Medal of Service in 2007 for the outstanding contribution to health care and education from the Canadian Association
   of Physicians of India Heritage.
10. Grant's Community Achiever Award in 2006 for his outstanding
    contribution in the field of public health.
11. Order of Ontario in 2005, Government of Ontario.
12. May Yoshida Award in 2005 by Centre for Equity in Health and
    Society.
13. Lifetime/Outstanding Achievement Award in 2005 by Indo-
    Canada Chamber of Commerce.
14. Senior Member Designate in 2003 by the Canadian Medical
    Association for lifetime services.

15. Honorary Life Membership: Ontario Medical Association, 2002.

16. Certificate of Recognition, City of Toronto Public Health Department, 2001.

17. The 25th Anniversary Race Relation Award by Urban Alliance on Race Relations 2000.

18. Eagle Feather Award: First Nations House Indigenous Students Services, the University of Toronto, 1999.

19. R D Defries Award and Honorary Life Membership, Canadian Public Health Association, 1999.

20. The John Hastings Award for Excellence in Service to the University and the Community, The Faculty of Medicine, University of Toronto, 1997.